LEARNING THEIR LANGUAGE

LEARNING THEIR LANGUAGE

LANGUAGE

Intuitive Communication
with
Animals and Nature

MARTA WILLIAMS

NEW WORLD LIBRARY
NOVATO, CALIFORNIA

New World Library
14 Pamaron Way
Novato, California 94949

Edited by Katharine Farnam Conolly and Carol Venolia
Cover design by Mary Ann Casler
Text design and typography by Tona Pearce Myers
Interior photograph on page 99 by Dominique Cognée

The material in this book is intended for education. No expressed or implied guarantee as to the effects of the use of the recommendations can be given nor liability taken.

Library of Congress Cataloging-in-Publication Data
Williams, Marta
    Learning their language : intuitive communication with animals and nature / by Marta Williams.
        p.   cm.
Includes bibliographical references.
ISBN 978-1-57731-243-7 (pbk. : alk. paper)
1. Pets—Behavior. 2. Human-animal communication. 3. Animal communication.
4. Human-animal relationships. I. Title.
SF412.5.W57 2003
636.088'7—dc21   2003000164

First Printing, May 2003
ISBN 978-1-57731-243-7
Printed in Canada on acid-free, partially recycled paper

20 19 18 17 16 15 14 13 12

I wrote this book for the Earth's animals, all the plants and the forests, the rivers and mountains, the wild and beautiful places, and the spirit of the Earth herself. They all want us to hear them again, as did our ancestors, and to welcome their voices on the council. I hope that in some way I will help to make this come about.

Contents

Acknowledgments

Virginia Simpson-Magruder, thank you so much for setting this process in motion. If it weren't for you, I'd still be scratching my head wondering how to get a book published. May the red-tailed hawks visit you daily and may magic be always with you.

Certain members of my family are, I'm sure, hoping that I never decide to write another book. Thank you to my parents, Jean and John Williams, and my sister, Anne Millington, for their tireless editing. I promise that if I ever do this again I will hire help.

The people at New World Library have been a pleasure to work with. I extend gratitude to everyone on the staff and particularly to my editor, Georgia Hughes, for her support and expert guidance and insight, and to Munro Magruder for his creativity and enthusiasm in promoting this book.

Thanks to all my clients, colleagues, and students over the years — both animals and people — who have supported my work. Special gratitude to Sylvie Maier, Petra and Freek Gout, Ellen Spiegel, Sam Louie, Janet Shepherd, Marla Williams, Madeline Yamate, Tina Hutton, Carol Gurney, Barbara Chasteen, Diana Thompson and all those who offered their stories for inclusion in these pages. Thanks also to my animals for their love and support.

Foreword

Animals have a unique way of affecting our hearts. They sidle in closer than humans do, opening us up emotionally and allowing us to confide our deepest thoughts, feelings, and aspirations. A nuzzle, a lick, a meow, or a rub can bring a smile and make our day.

Some of us talk to our animal friends as if they completely understand what we are saying — and, possibly because of this, they do. People who have not had the pleasure of living with animals think we're nuts. Yet human-animal communication transcends the limits of the spoken word; it has a feeling of mutual respect and caring. Animals allow us to be ourselves without shame, embarrassment, or doubt.

I've practiced veterinary medicine for twenty-five years, and holistic veterinary healing for twenty-three of those. During this time, I've experienced amazing interactions between animals and their human caretakers. Most people who live with animals have ongoing conversations with these friends. When I lost my cat friend, Hollywood, I began talking to myself whenever I was home alone — filling the gap where my furry buddy used to be.

While I've always communicated with animals, especially those who come to me for healing, I never really thought about it consciously. So when Marta Williams asked me to write a preface for her book, I was excited about doing so.

Marta has written a very basic, loving instruction book. It is filled with stories about her animal and human clients, along with step-by-step procedures for understanding and speaking with animals — whether or not you are already acquainted with those animals. It gives credence to all the times when you've said something to your horse, cat, or dog, and felt them reply in kind.

This book has helped me to slow down and remember to ask my animal patients how they feel and whether they want my help. I let them know that I will be as gentle with them as possible, and that in order to begin any healing process they have to be part of it; it's a partnership. Communicating these things to them is as important as any medical treatment. Without communication and permission, stressful situations can occur, diluting any beneficial result. Conscious communication helps promote understanding between me and my patients. It is unbelievably rewarding to ask an animal for help, and then see him acknowledge this by doing what I asked.

A few days ago, I was examining a dog patient for a colleague of mine. This is an older dog who is usually uncooperative. In fact, my colleague carries scars on his arm from an attempt at opening the dog's mouth to see his tongue — a part of diagnosis in the practice of Traditional Chinese Veterinary Medicine. When the dog walked in, I had no knowledge of his past behavior. So while meeting him and finding out what was wrong, I asked him to open his mouth. His human caretaker almost fell off her seat when the dog simply yawned, showing me his tongue.

Another time I was attempting to help a horse named Sam, whose neck was bothering him. He had difficulty bending to one side, and nobody had taken the time to ask him what was wrong or if they might help. When I approached Sam, he was in the pasture, not the slightest bit interested in getting caught with a halter and lead rope. So I stayed where I was, about twenty yards away. I told him I had noticed that his neck seemed to hurt and asked him if he wanted my help. I just stayed there, and after a few minutes he approached me, bowing his head for me to put the halter on.

Working in partnership with animals is always more effective than the human-dominant model. One day, my good horse pal and teacher, Louie the thoroughbred, was teaching me about trotting, changing directions, and moving forward in general until he did not want to move forward with me on his back. When I asked Louie to trot, he would trot for a few steps, then he would slow to a walk or he would stop as if he were caught in quicksand. He then decided he was not going to move forward at all, and, try as I might, I could not move him. What was he saying? At the same time, I was having difficulty moving forward emotionally in my life. Could Louie be responding to my mood via some type of body language?

The next time I visited Louie, I was in a better emotional space, again moving forward in my life. This was also a time when Louie's caretaker was out of town and we were able to communicate more clearly. I asked Louie how he was feeling, and he said he wanted to get outside the arena. So I haltered him and walked up and down the driveway hill, allowing him to enjoy the view and eat young weeds along the way. When we returned to his arena home, I asked him what he felt like doing next. In response, he walked across the arena where we usually worked and began doing figure-eights on his own. He seemed to be saying, "You gave me what I wanted; now it's time to work." Episodes like this enrich the life we share with our animal friends.

Marta Williams is a gifted animal intuitive who gives us, in this book, a way of deepening our relationships with animals. Through her use of simple terms and easy exercises, she helps us link our beings with those of our animal friends, allowing us to grow spiritually. She brings hope and love to these relationships. As you read this book, prepare to open your mind and heart — and to learn their language.

— Cheryl Schwartz, D.V.M.,
Author of *Four Paws, Five Directions:
A Guide to Chinese Medicine for Cats & Dogs*
January 31, 2003

Author's Note to Text

I tried wherever possible to avoid using the pronoun "it" when referring to an animal. Animals are not inanimate objects and they do have gender, but which gender pronoun to use when either would do? The convention is to use "he" in these cases. Instead, I decided to use "he" and "she" alternately, chapter by chapter. I also tried not to objectify animals by using the word "owner" when referring to the human side of an animal-human relationship. Instead, I use the term, the "animal's person" or the "animal's people."

Introduction

All Our
Relations

W hen I first met Whiskers, a young black mustang horse, she
was frightened of everything and could not be handled. It
was impossible to wash her, put on a fly mask (a protective face
screen that wards off flies), or safely lead her around the stable. No
one knew exactly what had happened to her, but she must have
been severely abused, judging by her behavior. As I talked with her
using the silent language of intuition, she told me her story. She
showed me images of her mother being killed by the men who
captured them. Then I saw images of these men teasing and taunt-
ing Whiskers because she was so scared and reactive. I got an overwhelming feeling of loneliness and dread, as well as profound grief
over the loss of her mother. She explained that she could no longer
trust people, and I understood why perfectly.

What could I do for this little mare who'd been so ill-treated by humans? I sent her feelings of love and images of a possible future in which she could be happy and safe. I told her that what happened to her was wrong; no horse should have to endure that. I promised her that she would always stay with her current people and would never be treated poorly again. She asked for a new name, and the name "Sadie" came to my mind — so that's who she became.

Sadie needed what any human would need in that situation: someone to listen to her story, give her support, and reassure her about the future so that she could begin to let go of her grief, anger, and fear. Then she could allow caring people to offer her a new life. After our conversation, Sadie started trusting again. The next morning she let her person put on a fly mask for the first time. It was possible for me to help Sadie because I had learned to speak her language — intuitive communication, the language of all life.

That day when Sadie and I talked, she and I mentally exchanged thoughts, feelings, and pictures, which is how intuitive communication works. I relied completely on my intuition or inner knowledge to send and receive information mentally. The term "animal communication" is commonly used to describe this ability to talk silently. In this book, I use the term "intuitive communication," which not only includes the ability to communicate this way with animals, but also applies to silent communication with all living beings. While you can talk silently with everything from fireflies to mountain lions, you can also talk with plants, rivers, mountains, and the elements and forces of nature.

I know this sounds implausible, and I don't expect you to believe it without proof. For myself, I've collected enough verified anecdotal evidence, working mainly with animals, that I am now certain the ability exists. I have proven to myself that it's real. That's what I hope to help you do.

People of indigenous cultures see intuitive communication as normal human behavior. To them, animals, plants, and the features of the land are relatives; every form of life has feelings, intelligence, spirit, and the ability to communicate, regardless of form and species. You can see this attitude in the words of a holy woman of the Wintu tribe of California, commenting on the destruction of nature brought about by the Gold Rush in that state:

> The white people never cared for land or deer or bear. When we Indians kill meat, we eat it all up. When we dig roots we make little holes. When we build houses, we make little holes. When we burn grass for grasshoppers, we don't ruin things. We shake down acorns and pine nuts. We don't chop down the trees. We only use dead wood. But the white people plow up the ground, pull down the trees, kill everything. The tree says, "No. I am sore. Don't hurt me." But they chop it down and cut it up. The spirit of the land hates them. They blast out trees and stir it up to its depths. They saw up the trees. That hurts them. The Indians never hurt anything, but the white people destroy all. They blast rocks and scatter them on the ground. The rock says, "Don't. You are hurting me." But the white people pay no attention. When the Indians use rocks, they take little round ones for their cooking. How can the spirit of the earth like the white man? Everywhere the white man has touched it, it is sore.[1]

Walking Buffalo (Tatanga Mani), a Stoney Indian of Alberta, was educated in white man's schools but never gave up his relationship with nature. At the age of eighty-seven, in a speech he gave in London in the late 1960s, he described his ability to talk to trees:

> Did you know that trees talk? Well they do. They talk to each other, and they'll talk to you if you listen. Trouble is, white people don't listen. They never learned to listen to the Indians so I don't suppose they'll listen to other voices in nature. But I have learned a lot from trees: sometimes about the weather, sometimes about animals, sometimes about the Great Spirit.[2]

One does not have to go back in time to find evidence of people relating to nature in this way. The beliefs expressed by the Wintu holy woman and Walking Buffalo are common in contemporary indigenous cultures throughout the world. Even though modern humans are now alienated from nature, this silent communication with other life forms appears to be our true heritage.

A contemporary example of this relationship can be seen in the U'wa, a tribe who have lived in the cloud forests of the Colombian Andes for thousands of years. The U'wa are now threatened by development; Occidental Petroleum has been exploring for oil on U'wa tribal lands. Oil extraction would result in destruction of the region and the U'wa way of life. At one point, the U'wa vowed to commit collective suicide if the project went forward, because they view death as preferable to watching the destruction of their homeland. They believe that oil is the blood running through the veins of the earth. In their words:

> Oil is the blood of Mother Earth ... to take the oil is, for us, worse than killing your own mother. If you kill the Earth, then no one will live.[3]

If humans hope to survive and thrive on this earth, we will
have to relearn how to live in partnership with all other life forms.
Our beliefs about animals and the natural world must shift to
something more like those of our ancestors and contemporary
indigenous people. Learning intuitive communication helps make
this possible.

There is tremendous power in being able to communicate
intuitively with animals and nature — a power to help stop
destruction and bring protection and positive change. The U'wa
reconsidered their original plan for dealing with the oil companies
and devised a new strategy. They decided to talk to the oil and tell
it to "move" and hide from the oil company drills. I recently read
that Occidental Petroleum, the multinational oil company doing
the exploratory drilling, announced that it was relinquishing control of the U'wa ancestral lands after company oil exploration last
summer came up dry.[4] That kind of collaboration to protect
nature becomes possible once you have the ability to communicate intuitively with other life forms.

When you are just beginning to practice intuitive communication, it's easiest to work with domesticated animals rather than
wild animals or nature. That way you can check on the accuracy
of the information you receive intuitively. For example, you could
ask a friend to give you some questions about her animal. The
questions need to be verifiable and the answers unknown to you.
You could ask questions like, "Do you like children?" or, "Do you
like other animals?" You need to select questions with unpredictable answers, so that you won't be able to make a logical guess.
After you ask the questions of the animal, ask your friend to verify your results. When you've been accurate at this several times, it
starts to sink in that your ability is real.

In communicating intuitively you will not just be reading an animal's body language or making educated guesses. Intuitive communication is something completely different. To be successful at it, you have to partition off your rational mind and rely exclusively on your intuition to send and receive data. The process is simple, but it's such a departure from our conditioning and training that it can be difficult. Your mind may resist. In the beginning, I had a hard time mastering the technique or believing that what I was receiving was real. I was only finally able to convince myself of my ability when I began doing repeated verifiable practice.

For example, when I asked Jake, a quarter horse, about his past experiences, he told me that he'd started out in Oregon on a cattle ranch where he was worked very hard. When he couldn't run cattle anymore, he became the backyard horse of a little girl with long blonde hair whom he had loved. Jake's current person knew his history and confirmed that what he conveyed (using mental pictures, words, and feelings) was accurate.

I now have so many verified cases like this that I know without doubt that intuitive communication is real. Something I once thought of as science fiction or magic, I now know to be a practical tool that can be very useful, especially for helping animals.

One of the most important services I now offer is assistance in finding lost animals. Take the case of Lexi, a female cat who was lost in upstate New York during a snowstorm. Lexi's person was convinced that her cat was dead or dying, but when I got in touch with Lexi she gave me the impression that she was somewhere warm. Then she sent a picture of a green apartment building and the knowledge that she was under something metal. She also showed me which direction to go to find her, starting from the woman's apartment. As soon as we got off the phone, the woman went out and found Lexi in exactly the spot described, curled up nice and cozy in a heating vent.

People often refer to my ability to communicate with animals as a gift. While I certainly see the ability to communicate intuitively as a gift, I do not consider myself to be gifted. Everyone has this gift of intuitive communication; we're just unaware of it. As young children we communicated this way with animals and nature quite naturally, but as we grew up we were discouraged from using imagination or following intuition, and eventually the ability became dormant. One of my students even remembers the precise moment when she stopped communicating this way with animals. She was walking to school one day at about age eight and saw some birds on the grass. She realized that she couldn't hear the birds speaking to her anymore and said to herself, "Oh, that must mean I'm growing up!"

When you are relearning and recovering this skill, checking your accuracy becomes crucial. You have to be able to prove to yourself that this is not just make-believe. Sometimes you can't verify the information you receive and your proof can only come in the form of the results you get. A positive change in the behavior or demeanor of the animal you are working with suggests that your communication was accurate and real.

The following story from Karen Berke, an accomplished student of animal communication, is an example of this, Karen wrote:

My horse had an injury to his right hip when he was only three years old, and it showed up when he was ridden at a canter (a running gait). As several trainers described it, his canter to the right, with the right front foot leading, was smooth while the canter to the left, with the left foot leading, was choppy and bumpy. It was very hard for me not to get off balance when cantering on the left lead and it was always a struggle for both of us. After one such frustrating evening, I was about to give up and just never try to canter to the left. Instead, I decided to ask my horse for help. Immediately, I mentally heard these words: "Sit up straight on your right side and put more weight in your right seatbone to balance yourself on me." I took a deep breath, did what he said, and found that it worked perfectly. From then on, I was able to ride the canter on his bad side without a problem.

Most of us have been taught that only humans are rational and that animals do not have sophisticated emotions the way we do. The idea that other aspects of nature could be sentient is simply not entertained. My experience with animals and nature contradicts this; I am certain that animals are as complex as we are and that there is intelligence and spiritual awareness in every form of life on the earth. By now I have consulted with thousands of animals whose lives have improved once their people addressed the emotional needs the animals revealed to me.

A student of mine had such an experience when working with a white male cat she was caring for at an animal shelter. The cat had been at the shelter for some time and was beginning to look scruffy and unhappy. She interviewed the cat using her newly acquired skills in intuitive communication, and he told her that he was depressed because he could not go out in the sun and was not going to be adopted. When she asked why he felt that way, he said that two people had been standing by his cage and had said that, because he was white, he would get sick in the sun, would be unable to go outside, and would not be adopted by anyone because no one would want such a cat.

The student asked around and found out that some shelter personnel had in fact had this discussion while standing in front of the cat's cage a few weeks earlier. The student immediately went to the cat and told him that he was a lovely cat who could go outside in the sun as long as someone put protective cream on his nose. She advised him that he would just have to work on finding a person who would be willing to do that for him every day. The cat reportedly perked up right away and started grooming himself. When people walked by his cage, he came forward to greet them. Within a week, he was adopted by someone who found him beautiful and had no problem with the task of putting sunscreen on his nose every day.

Sometimes a problem behavior, perceived to be emotional in nature, actually has a physical basis; this can often be determined by getting the animal's point of view. For example, Terry Link called to ask me to find out why Tequila, a buckskin quarter horse, was behaving badly. She, loved Tequila, but she was being told that he had a bad attitude that would only get worse, and that he should be sold. She telephoned me, gave me Tequila's name and description, and I went to work. When I got in touch with him intuitively, he sent me the distinct words, "My rib is out; it hurts!" Then he sent me a mental picture of him pointing with his nose to his left side around the area of the fourth rib.

When Terry called me for my report, I told her what I'd learned, cautioning that the information was just my intuitive impression and that she should get her chiropractor to check it out. That evening, I got a call from the chiropractor, who was astounded; the fourth rib on Tequila's left side was indeed out. The chiropractor wanted to know how I could have figured that out at a distance of more than one thousand miles without even seeing a picture of the horse. I told him that I used my intuition and would be happy to teach him how to do it too, as I am certain that anyone can learn to do what I do. After the treatment, Tequila went back to being a calm, pleasant horse.

This dynamic occurs in all domesticated animals; problem behaviors are often caused by unaddressed physical discomfort. When animals have a physical problem, they try to tell us about it intuitively. If we don't get their message, they start to act out to get us to address the problem. Cats and dogs may begin eliminating on floors or furniture, or they may become aggressive for no obvious reason. You should always check with a veterinarian to determine whether there is a physical cause for bad behaviors. But if the cause isn't physical, intuitive communication may help resolve the situation. Until you learn to do this yourself, you may want to employ the services of a professional animal communicator.

Even though we no longer freely communicate with other life forms, as did our indigenous ancestors, the door to intuitive communication is still open to us. Being able to communicate this way is as much a part of being human as our ability to see or hear. To reawaken your intuition and your ability to communicate, all you need to do is study and practice. Anyone who has the desire to learn can excel at intuitive communication. Since the ability is innate, I have only to teach you how to recapture, consciously use, and perfect it. That's what I hope to do in this book.

This is a step-by-step guide to developing your ability to communicate intuitively. Even if you live on an isolated island in Alaska and can only get out by ferry, you can take this book and learn to communicate with animals and nature all on your own. You will not need to find practice partners or form a study group, although that can be helpful. I designed the exercises to be fun and easy. Many are verifiable, so you can get feedback on your accuracy. For some of the exercises, you will need to work with your friends' or acquaintances' animals in order to get verification of your results.

Once you've had some practice with other people's animals, I will teach you how to use these skills to hear what your own animals have to say. Ironically, it's more difficult to work with your own animals. Because you already know so much about them, it's harder to be objective and you can easily end up feeling like you are just making things up. I've included detailed guidance on how to deal with the blocks you may encounter in the learning process. I've also included a section on communicating and collaborating with wildlife, the plants in your garden, and the natural landscape.

This book is very practical, giving you lots of exercises and experiments to try. In my experience, intuitive communication is best learned by doing. Through repeated verifiable exercises, I was able to prove to myself that intuitive communication is real. You will need to prove this to yourself, too, and these exercises will help you do that. After you begin doing the exercises, you may find that you want to practice with animals you see on your walks, at the barn, or at a friend's house, so get a sturdy notebook to take with you for your practice. If you want to build your confidence in intuitive communication, it's essential to record your results and look back on your progress.

In Part One of the book, I will tell how I got involved in this work. I'll explain in detail what intuitive communication is, discuss the question of accuracy, and give some anecdotes to support my claims. Throughout the book, I've included my case studies and the many stories I've been told by clients, students, and colleagues.

In Part Two, I will describe a new way to convey information to your animals that will improve relationships and help solve problems. Then I'll teach you the basic techniques for receiving information intuitively from an animal, which is of course more challenging. You will start with basic exercises and learn methods for dealing with any internal blocks that may get in your way.

Part Three will help you refine your technique and get comfortable with the process of interviewing an animal using intuitive communication skills. Once you have some confidence, you can begin to apply your skills.

In Part Four, you will learn to communicate with your own animals and receive suggestions for making intuitive communication part of your everyday life. You will practice questioning a sick or injured animal about her symptoms, and you will learn how to ask an unknown animal about her previous people and experiences. If you wish, you may try your hand at locating a lost animal and communicating with the spirit of an animal that has died.

Part Five teaches you how to use your skills to communicate with all life forms, including wild animals, plants, rivers, and mountains. There are also some suggested experiments for using intuition to collaborate with the natural world and the spirit of the earth herself to restore the health of the planet.

I hope that as we recover our ability to communicate with animals and the rest of nature, we will learn once again to live in balance with these, our relations.

Part One

The World
of Intuitive
Communication

Chapter One

How I Learned to Communicate Intuitively

I did not grow up consciously able to talk intuitively with animals. I learned how to do this by studying and practicing, just as you can. I don't believe that I have any more innate talent for it than you do. For more than a decade, I've taught classes in intuitive communication, and I have yet to meet someone who was incapable of learning. The only difference between me and a beginning student, is the amount of time I've spent practicing and researching.

I have, however, been concerned about animals and nature for as long as I can remember, which led to my pursuit of an undergraduate degree in resource conservation at the University of California, Berkeley. While in college, I developed a severe back problem. It was so bad that I had to take a break from school. Rather than getting back surgery, I sought out noninvasive alternative therapies, which put me in touch with a different crowd than I was meeting in my university classes. Had I not been exposed to alternative forms of healing — bodyworkers, psychic healers, and the like — I might not have been so accepting of the idea of intuitive communication when I encountered it later on.

At one of the healing workshops I attended, something happened that changed my life: I learned about the work of J. Allen Boone. One of the people at the workshop suggested that I read Boone's book, *Kinship with All Life*. When I went looking for the book, I found that it was out of print. I finally located a dusty original hardbound copy in the stacks of a public library. The inside back cover indicated that it had last been checked out in 1954. Boone's books have since been reprinted[1] and are available in most bookstores, but back then few people seemed to know of him.

Reading this book changed my whole perspective on what was real and possible. In his book, Boone told how he came to know a famous Hollywood German shepherd dog named Strongheart. Boone had been asked to take care of the dog for several months. During that time, he realized that Strongheart was far more intelligent than he was, and furthermore that Strongheart understood everything Boone said, felt, or thought. With this insight, Boone set out to hear responses back from Strongheart so that they could converse — and he succeeded. The book is elegant and convincing, but no one would ever be able to figure out Boone's technique from his book. Even so, he persuaded me that intuitive communication was real. Up until that point I knew it only as an intriguing daydream and the subject of some of my favorite science fiction novels.

One thing I found compelling about Boone was that he voiced an ethic and a philosophy that I was not seeing reflected anywhere in society. Boone talked about the equality of all living beings and advised that all life, regardless of its form, would respond favorably to our genuine interest and respect. To Boone, there were no communication boundaries between one life form and another; the silent language he discovered with Strongheart had the power to unite us all.

After I finished my studies at Berkeley, I worked as a director of wildlife rehabilitation clinics for about five years. Even though this was important work, and it was fantastic to interact with wild animals every day, I worried about the problems facing the animals and the earth, and wanted to help in a more significant way. Hoping that I could have a greater impact as a professional scientist, I earned an M.S. degree in biology at San Francisco State University. I conducted my thesis research at the U.S. Fish and Wildlife Kesterson Reservoir in central California, studying the harmful effects of chemical residues from agricultural runoff on birds' reproductive systems. Many birds in the Kesterson refuge were born disfigured, and none of the juveniles survived to adulthood.

After graduate school, I went to work in the field of environmental regulation and restoration, conducting audits, hazardous-waste site clean-ups, and habitat restoration projects. This work was worthwhile too, but I still felt like I wasn't doing enough, or wasn't doing the *right* thing. My work as an environmental scientist seemed to be too little, too late. In my free time, I was an environmental activist (and still am), but even that felt inadequate.

In the late 1980s, I decided to go on a vision quest.[2] I had been reading and hearing a lot about impending changes to the earth's climate and ecology, caused by human activity. The Hopi prophecies for our time suggested that if people could experience a shift in consciousness and reconnect with animals, nature, and spirit, much of the predicted destruction could be avoided.[3] I started thinking about how such a connection could be encouraged in the modern world. I decided to go on the vision quest to ask to be shown the best way for me to help this change come about.

During the trip to the vision quest site in the White Mountains in California, the trip leaders told me about a woman in my region who offered classes in animal communication. I became very intrigued by the idea that I could actually study and learn how to do this. Throughout my time in the desert, I could not stop thinking about it. I had the feeling I was being led to do this.

As soon as I returned from the vision quest, I signed up for classes and started reading everything I could find on the subject of animal communication. I soon realized that this pursuit was not going to be that easy. In fact, I had a hard time learning to do animal communication, mainly because I believed that I was making things up, and therefore I felt like a failure.

It didn't help that whenever I told people outside of the animal communication classes what I was doing, their reactions were negative and guarded. At that time, in the late 1980s, most people regarded intuitive communication with animals as unintelligent nonsense. As a scientist, I was accustomed to being taken seriously, not ridiculed. In addition to regaining the actual skill of intuitive communication, I had to learn how to deal with the taboos associated with this field and to remain confident in the face of doubt and disbelief from those around me. I now see that process as having been immensely valuable; I had to learn to trust my own truth in order to claim this skill. Those negative experiences were also good, in a way, because they motivated me to find easier, more effective ways to help others learn.

One day, a turning point in my studies occurred. I was living with a friend who was somewhat skeptical about animal communication. At the time I had several cats, including my brindle cat, Jenny. When I came home that day, my friend said, "OK, if you can do this stuff then tell me what Jenny did today." He had been home all day and had observed Jenny's activities.

I went to Jenny, closed my eyes, and mentally asked, "Jenny, what did you do today?" Immediately, I received a picture of Jenny up on the ledge of my backyard fence, touching noses with a squirrel who was also standing on the fence ledge. I had never seen anything like that before; I thought that it was very odd and probably wrong, but that I would say it anyway. I told my friend the picture Jenny had sent me. His jaw dropped and his eyes widened as he said, "Oh my God!" Then he confirmed that what I "saw" had actually happened. I had my first undeniable verification that intuitive communication was accurate and real and that I could do it.

My friend continued, "Ask her what they were talking about!" So I did. This time she sent me pictures and words. She said that she'd told the squirrel to watch out for my other cats, who were mean and who would hurt the squirrel. She said that she and the squirrel were talking about the squirrel's babies, and then she sent me two pictures — one of walnuts and one of laundry hanging on a line. From those pictures, I presume that Jenny and the squirrel also talked about nuts and laundry.

At this point in my life, I began practicing in earnest. I organized a practice group of students from the class I was taking. I talked intuitively to every animal that crossed my path. I would ask wild animals about their habits, then look up the responses in my field books to see if the answers I received were right. I would interview dogs in the park, then strike up a casual conversation with their people to discover whether the information was correct. Each time I had any doubts, I soon had another confirming experience.

One day, I went to the home of one of my activist friends to talk with her dog. This woman was skeptical, too, but she wanted to see what I could do. After some inconclusive questions and results, she suggested that I ask her dog about her favorite activities. When I asked this question, the dog flashed me a mental picture of herself sitting in a chair wearing a party hat, seated at a table with lots of other dogs sitting in chairs wearing hats, and there was a big carrot cake in the middle of the table.

You can imagine what went on internally as I debated whether to tell this woman the picture I'd received. I knew that I didn't make it up; I had never even heard of dog birthday parties at that time. I decided that if I wanted to do intuitive communication, I was going to have to say what I got no matter what the consequences and no matter how foolish I might appear (one of many challenges in doing this work!). So I told her, and she said, "Oh yes, we give her a birthday party every year and invite all her dog friends and give them a carrot cake. Yes, they have hats and sit at the table. But I'm still not convinced that this stuff works." Well, no matter; I was convinced!

I began working part-time as an animal communicator, teaching classes and helping people with their animals in private consultations. Eventually, I switched to doing it full-time.

I have seen that once people experience intuitive communication with animals, their perception of the world changes. Each animal on earth becomes an individual with the same qualities of sentience, emotion, and spirit that humans have. Once you have really communicated with animals, it is impossible to go back to thinking of them as inferior or limited.

In the 1980s, when I started studying animal communication, few people knew about it and practitioners were scoffed at. Today there are thousands of people learning animal communication and millions who have heard of it throughout the world. It is on the news, both in the newspapers and on TV. I am greatly encouraged by the fact that animal sentience is being so widely accepted, even though traditional science continues to question its validity. What is needed now is for many more people to take enlightened action on behalf of the animals and the earth.

Chapter Two

Intuition:
The Hidden Ability

Everyone has intuitive ability, but most of us are unaware of it. We use our intuition daily, but at an unconscious level. Anyone can learn how to bring intuitive ability under conscious control. Some people do this easily with minimal instruction.

One of my clients, Linda Stine, is a case in point. She saw the information on my Web site, read a few of the books I recommended, and then was easily able to communicate intuitively with her quarter horse gelding, Zip. She shared the following story:

> My newly acquired horse, Zip, injured himself in the pasture. He had a cut from the bulb of his heel to the fetlock joint. The wound healed well after two weeks, but he remained lame. After five weeks I had the vet come out again, but all he could suggest was to do nerve blocking to isolate the problem area. I decided against that and had

a talk with Zip instead. I told him I just wanted to know where it hurt and why, since he appeared to be completely healed. I told him I only wanted to help him. Later, I was walking past his pasture when all of a sudden it came to me so clearly: I saw a picture of him doing barrel racing. At the same time I was seeing this image, I felt pain, fear, frustration, and anger very strongly. I got an overall message that Zip did not want our relationship to be like that.

I was overcome with emotion and said out loud, "No! No! No! I don't care if you ever run a barrel again. I will never treat you badly." Then I got a feeling that he was worried and that he didn't want to let me down or upset me to the point of my getting angry with him. I told him that all I wanted from him, what would make me happy, would be to see him playing free in his pasture. As soon as I said that to him, he went to the bottom of the hill in his pasture, rolled, and got up. Then he squealed, bucked, and galloped at full speed to the top of the hill. Zip has not taken one lame step since! We are now working on what Zip does want to do.

SUPPRESSING THE ABILITY

I have heard similar stories from many people. This is part of what convinces me that we all have an inborn intuitive ability. But this ability is suppressed early on by teachers, parents, and the general culture. The reasons for this are complex and, I believe, go far back in time. At this point, suppression of intuition has become a habit of our modern culture. People like Linda, on the other hand, may have grown up with someone who *encouraged* the use of intuition.

Intuition is a function of the right side of the brain, the side associated with creativity and emotion. It is the antithesis of logic and it comes to us from inside, from our sixth sense. Unless there is some kind of physical damage to the body, everyone has an inborn intuitive sense. As children, we used it freely. We didn't worry whether something was illogical or silly; we acted spontaneously. We were good at receiving intuitive information and communicating with animals. But as we grew up, we were trained to disconnect from our core selves and be critical of intuitive, non-logical information — to consciously screen it out. As adults, we still receive intuitive data and often act upon it, but this all occurs on a subconscious or unconscious basis.

Because we have learned so well to suppress our intuition, it usually only emerges in a crisis. One of my clients told me a story that illustrates this. One day when she was driving to work, she kept seeing an image in her mind's eye of the underside of her dining room table. She thought this was odd and tried to ignore it, but the image had a quality of urgency about it. She thought perhaps there was something wrong at her house — a fire or something — so she turned around and went home to check. When she got there, she found her cat lying on his back having a seizure; his gaze was locked on the underside of the dining room table.

This was a classic example of intuition; there was no rational process involved, no deductive or inductive reasoning, no educated guesses — nothing. She could not have received that picture in her mind by any logical means, yet the picture was accurate. The only explanation is that the information came to her intuitively. By now I have heard so many stories like this from my clients and students — about how someone in their family knew intuitively from a distance the precise moment when another family member or pet became ill, was injured, or was dying — that I imagine it is quite common.

INTUITION IN DAILY LIFE

Unconsciously, we use intuition every day. We use it to scope out new people or situations, to figure out what to do when there is no logical course of action, and to feel out the safety of a situation that may have some unpredictable consequences. As children, we perfected the art of scoping out how someone else feels by tuning in to our parents; it was important for us to know how those adults who were our source of survival were feeling. A classic example of intuition is a mother's connection to her baby, knowing exactly what the baby needs even when separated. You are probably using your intuition more than you think.

You may be one of those people who knows who is on the phone before you pick it up; that's intuition. Or you may think of someone and then call, only to find out that he was thinking of you, too; that's intuition. Intuition is any hunch or gut feeling you get. You are using your intuition any time there is ambiguity and you rely on your gut feeling or instincts to decide which way to go, which person to see, which thing to select, or which approach is best.

INTUITION IQ TEST

Take the following intuition IQ test to see how well developed your intuitive ability is. Answer the following questions with the number that corresponds to one of the following frequencies. As you read each question, be aware that the ability identified in the question is an innate intuitive ability that you probably already possess even if you are not consciously aware of it.

0 — never
1 — sometimes
2 — frequently

1. Have you ever thought of a person and then gotten a call or message from them shortly thereafter?
2. Have you ever known (without logical explanation) who was calling before you picked up the phone?
3. Can you accurately guess someone else's emotion?
4. Can you accurately guess an animal's emotion?
5. Have you ever felt wary of a person or situation (for no apparent reason) and later found out that your wariness was justified?
6. Did you ever hear an animal talking to you mentally or see a picture sent to you by an animal in your mind's eye?
7. Did you ever hear a person talking to you mentally or see a picture sent to you by a person in your mind's eye?
8. Have you ever undeniably felt an emotion sent to you by an animal?
9. Have you ever undeniably felt an emotion sent to you by a person?
10. Are your first impressions usually accurate?
11. Did you ever get a strong (but not logical) feeling that you should (or shouldn't) do something and then found out that your feeling was accurate?
12. Were you ever sure that someone was lying to you (without any such outward signs), and later found out that you were right?
13. Did you ever know that something unpredictable was going to happen or realize it as it happened far away from you? (This includes knowing of an impending death.)
14. Have you ever felt that some unseen force intervened

to protect you from danger (e.g., detained you so that you avoided an accident)?

15. Do you ever have predictive dreams?

16. Do you ever feel a person's (or animal's) physical pain and symptoms of illness in your own body? (If yes, make sure you read chapter 12.)

17. Are people's motives always clear to you?

18. Do you feel that you have internal guidance in your life?

19. Do you tend to get a lot of hunches, gut feelings, and impressions about things (even if you ignore them)?

20. Are there a lot of coincidences in your life?

Add up your total score and see where you are in terms of your intuitive skill level.

0–13 Your intuition is in more of a dormant stage. It is there and you have the skill, so don't worry; intuition is a natural ability. You may have had a lot of conditioning in your life to be logical and rational and to ignore your feelings or hunches. Possibly intuition was actively discouraged for whatever reasons when you were growing up. Or you may have learned to be a very hard taskmaster on yourself, thus inhibiting your intuitive ability. This just means that you will have to work a little harder than someone who was encouraged to be intuitive as a child — or who was left to his or her own devices. You will especially want to work with the techniques described in chapter 7: The Critic Within.

14–27 Your intuitive skill is well developed and you are

using it in your everyday life, though you may not be highly aware of it. You could have trouble believing in your ability, but you are obviously making accurate assessments based on your intuition. You may benefit from the techniques described in chapter 7, which are designed to help you build your confidence in using your intuition in a more conscious, controlled way.

28–40   You have a highly developed intuitive ability and are probably aware of it. Sometimes people in this category are uncomfortable with their intuitive ability. You may need to study the techniques in this book for getting more control over how you use your intuition so that you run it rather than allowing it to run you. It is likely that you had someone in your life who was a role model for intuition or who encouraged you to be intuitive. You may also have had some significant experience in your life that opened you to your intuition.

DEFINITIONS

The term "intuition" covers a lot of territory. It has the same meaning as the word "psychic" (when both are used as adjectives), but "intuition" is more comfortable for many people. "Intuition" refers to any extrasensory perception: something you perceive independently from the five physical senses of sight, sound, touch, smell, and taste. Extrasensory perceptions parallel the physical senses. For example, you can see things intuitively, but you will see them in your mind's eye as a mental image or visualization, not as an actual image that your eyes directly perceive. When you communicate intuitively, you will be using one or more of the following extrasensory perceptions:

- Clairvoyance: This literally means "clear seeing." In intuitive communication, it refers to the ability to see images and pictures in your mind's eye. It also refers to the ability to intuitively know something about the past, present, or future without any logical explanation as to why you would know it. You can use this intuitive sense to see things that are distant from you, such as the location of a lost animal. You can also use it to find out about an animal's past people and experiences. Clear-sightedness is the operant ability when a thought that turns out to be intuitive information just pops into your head — such as when you know who is calling on the telephone before you pick it up.

- Clairsentience: This means "clear feeling," and it refers to the ability to intuitively feel the emotions or physical feelings of another. Feeling someone else's feelings is also known as empathy. Sometimes when people do this, they may physically feel a pain in their own bodies or be overcome by an emotion they are picking up.

- Clairaudience: This means "clear hearing," and it refers to the ability to hear words and phrases in your mind's ear. This is also known as mental telepathy. When you hear this way, the words and phrases may sound like your own voice. Without doing some verifiable work, you might find it hard to believe that the words are actually coming from somewhere outside yourself.

- Clairalience: This means "clear smelling." It is an ability that surfaces less often, but some people are able to

get very clear impressions of smells. An example
would be asking a horse about her favorite treat and
then getting an impression of the smell of a carrot or
a pear.

- Clairhambience: This means "clear tasting," and it is
the ability to get intuitive impressions of taste. An
example would be asking a cat to tell you her favorite
food and getting an impression of the taste of fish.

A PROFILE OF THE INTUITIVE PERSON

People who do intuitive work for humans are called psychics or
intuitives. Medical intuitives relate their impressions about what is
going on with an individual physically or emotionally. People who
do intuitive work with animals are called animal communicators,
even though many of them, like me, communicate with other
aspects of nature as well.

In her book, *Your Sixth Sense*,[1] psychologist Belleruth
Naparstek interviewed more than forty well-known, well-
respected human intuitives. She concluded that people who excel
at intuition usually had a mentor or role model who assisted them.
In some cases, dramatic events — such as being in a car collision
— opened people up to their intuition. Also, severe trauma in
childhood was found to be a contributing factor for some intuitives, leading them to turn inward and rely on their own
resources. People raised in a culture that values intuition, as in
many of the contemporary indigenous cultures of the world, are
able to consciously tap into their intuition at all times.

Conversely, people who are raised to be extremely logical or
who work in such a field, or those who were taught that intuition
is negative or taboo for some reason, will be less likely to be skilled

at intuition — even though, like everyone, they have the innate ability. Naparstek is quick to point out that you don't have to have a near-death experience or be abused in order to be highly intuitive. Things that help focus the mind, such as yoga and meditation, will work just as well.

At present far more women are attracted to the field of intuition than men; most of my students are women. I don't think this is accidental. Probably most students of animal communication and intuitive ability are women. Men can learn intuitive skills just as well as women, and I think they have the same level of interest; they certainly love animals as much as women do. But I believe there is an extra societal barrier for men when it comes to exploring intuition. Men are trained from an early age to be logical and are expected to behave in a rational and objective manner whenever possible. That has become part of the definition of what it means to be male in many modern cultures. Women, on the other hand, are expected to be intuitive and illogical, and to have wide-ranging emotional states; that has become the cultural expectation for women. These roles are just cultural conventions, not biological facts, but they have been heavily reinforced. This makes it difficult for men to break the mold and do something as "silly," "frivolous," "sentimental," and "illogical" as studying animal communication. Classes that teach people how to use intuition to succeed in business, probably attract more male participants. Eventually this will even out as intuitive communication with animals and nature grows in popular acceptance.

SOCIAL TABOOS

Why is the term "psychic" received so negatively? While some psychics are not very competent, the same holds true for practitioners in every field. It does not explain the overwhelming taboo against the term; something else is going on. I recall a lost-dog case I worked on in which the breeder, a woman who lived in Alabama, had just placed the dog in a new home in North Carolina. Within one hour, the dog had escaped and was running amok, crossing five-lane highways and eluding capture. I was called in to help by the rescue people, not the breeder. When the breeder found out that they had called in a pet psychic, she was appalled. She chastised them for doing something so stupid and ridiculous. As it turned out, everything I reported about the dog's whereabouts, patterns, and attitude was accurate. Far from being worried, helpless, and lost — which was what everyone imagined — I sensed that the dog had established a territory and was traveling it in a wide circle. I saw him finding food easily and felt that he had decided to avoid people and just live on his own.

As the search progressed, it became apparent that my information was correct. I had also warned the dog to stay completely away from all roads, which he thereafter did. The breeder came to North Carolina to help with the search. Though skeptical, she went along with the search tactics I suggested. She got her dog back within a day; he just came up to her car in the middle of the night and jumped in. Afterward, she called me and told me (in a wonderful Alabama accent) that although she could not believe she was saying it, she was going to be my biggest fan for life. Something she had thought of as being absolute bunk turned out to be the key to finding her lost dog.

People who are legitimate psychics — those who have a track record of accuracy and a reputation for integrity — usually try to distance themselves from the term psychic. They prefer to be called intuitives because there is so much negativity associated with the term psychic. For this reason I, too, choose to call what I do intuitive rather than psychic communication. Some negativity is justified; there are some psychics who are inept and dishonest. Since becoming a psychic does not require a university degree, there are probably more incompetents in this field than in a more rigorous discipline. The Dial-a-Psychic infomercials don't help, either. But every field has practitioners who should be put out of business that somehow manage to keep hanging on. What is true for finding a psychic or intuitive to help you applies to any service industry: it's safest to ask around and go with a personal recommendation.

I suspect that some of the negative associations with the term "psychic" originate in historical periods when it was dangerous to be psychic because people were persecuted for doing divination or other activities that involved the use of psychic ability.

SCIENCE AND INTUITION

Scientists are some of the most vocal critics of psychic ability. In the early part of the twentieth century, scientists expended a great deal of energy trying to debunk practicing psychics. Contemporary scientists, with few exceptions, perfunctorily dismiss psychic or intuitive endeavors as insignificant and unworthy of study.

It is fortunate that within the last few decades, some scientists — particularly physicists — have started to take intuition (or "psi phenomena," as they call it) seriously. These scientists are now studying intuition using the scientific method. They are finding that everyone has a basic capacity for intuitive insight and that information obtained through the use of intuition can be highly accurate.

One of the most prolific researchers in this area is physicist Russell Targ. In the 1970s, with his colleague Charles Putoff,[2] Targ worked at the Stanford Research Institute conducting a study of human intuitive ability. In these experiments, the researchers worked with ordinary people of no professed intuitive talent, giving them brief instructions in how to do "remote viewing" — the military term for psychic or intuitive ability. At the time, military experiments focused on the ability to see intuitively, hence the emphasis on remote *viewing*.

In one experiment, the subjects were told that a member of the research team had just traveled to a nearby, undisclosed location. The subjects were asked to guess what this location looked like. They were told to draw and describe in words their most fleeting impressions of where the research team member might have gone and to withhold any attempt at analysis or interpretation. Often, the subjects were able to accurately describe or draw the exact location of the research member. The results proved that average people with very little training have innate intuitive ability. With training, some of these military remote viewers were able to consistently achieve a 75 percent accuracy rate.[3] Targ went on to work with the U.S. military to further study these intuitive abilities, asking test subjects to locate crashed planes and secret Soviet military installations.

Targ discusses his years of research on this subject in his recent work, *Miracles of the Mind.* He defines the ability to view remotely as an ability to tap into universal knowledge or the collective unconscious, which he terms "the nonlocal mind." He says, "This fascinating and not yet fully understood phenomenon that connects us to each other and to the world at large allows us to describe, experience, and influence activities occurring anywhere in space and time."[4]

The study of the nonlocal mind falls within the field of quantum physics. Targ cites credible experiments that prove the existence of quantum interconnectedness — the interrelatedness of all matter. By measuring the polarization of a pair of photons born in the same interaction but traveling in opposite directions, researchers determined that the polarization of one photon appears to be altered by the mere act of observing the other photon, even though they are traveling away from each other. As a result of these observations, physicists postulate that all matter is conscious, aware, and in communication with all other matter at all times. This dynamic, then, accounts for our ability to know at any given moment any piece of information we desire; all we need to do is tap into the collective mind or universal knowledge — what is known in the Hindu religion as the "akashic record."

In his book *Radical Nature*,[5] philosophy professor Christian de Quincey offers perhaps the best available analysis and explanation of this concept of the nonlocal mind. De Quincey expands upon this challenging argument that all matter has consciousness.

Gary Schwartz is another scientist who turned his attention to the study of intuition. He teaches psychology, medicine, neurology, psychiatry, and surgery at the University of Arizona. He received his doctorate from Harvard University and worked for some time at Yale University directing the Yale Psychophysiology Center and Behavioral Medicine Clinic. His current book, *The Afterlife Experiments: Breakthrough Scientific Evidence of Life after Death*,[6] is a narrative of his scientific research into this phenomenon. The experiments were designed with strict scientific experimental protocol and the results were statistically analyzed. In the experiments, accomplished intuitives were asked to "read" people unknown to them. The people being read could only respond with yes or no answers and were hidden from view. The experiments were conducted using increasingly rigorous and controlled conditions. Schwartz sought to show that separate intuitives independently arrived at the same data about a person being read. He also wanted to rule out any possibility of fraud. In an interview about the book,[7] he indicated that the results of the experiments he conducted convinced him that the intuitives in his study were accurate and genuine.

SCIENCE, ANIMALS, AND NATURE

People often think it ridiculous that animals can have feelings or that they might possess the ability to reason. We are taught not to anthropomorphize animals, and chided for ascribing emotional motives to an animal's behavior. Animals are to be seen as blindly acting out of instinct in all situations. Most animal lovers know this to be inaccurate. Yet even the most confirmed among that group usually has some degree of conditioned bias against other forms of life. Why is it that, unlike indigenous people, modern humans view animals and other life forms as inferior? Some who have researched this question point to the development of alphabets and written language and the concurrent demise of oral traditions as the essential point of departure between ancient and modern culture.[8] They argue that the development of written language inserted a wedge between humans and the rest of nature, leading to our current state of alienation. I find the explanation of archeologist Marija Gimbutas[9] more convincing. Gimbutas documents the rise and eventual dominance of a marauding culture, thought to be Kurdish in origin, that invaded Old Europe from the northern desert starting about 7,000 years ago. She identifies the impetus for this invasion as a severe drought in the north (documented in the archeological records) that led to a migration and conquest on the part of the drought survivors. This marauding culture superseded almost every aspect of the peaceful, egalitarian, nature-worshipping cultures that prevailed in Old Europe during prehistory. It eventually spread to other continents, shifting worldwide values and beliefs toward exploitation of animals and the rest of nature.[10]

Modern science institutionalized the lowered status of the natural world. The father of modern science, Francis Bacon, believed that nature should be man's slave.[11] René Descartes, another pillar of modern science, believed that animals were automatons that felt no pain and had no emotions.[12] In my experience, both at college and later as a professional scientist, I found that many scientists — particularly biologists — held a limited view of the capabilities of other life forms. They believed, for example, that only human beings could feel grief or joy, make tools, use complex language, or have altruistic motives for their behaviors.

A handful of scientists have challenged the status quo. In their excellent book on the emotional lives of animals, Jeffrey Masson and Susan McCarthy[13] make a strong case, using anecdotal data, for the existence of sophisticated emotions in animals. In story after story, about wild and domestic animals, told by both laypeople and scientists, the authors provide undeniable proof that animals can feel grief, joy, and anger just as deeply as we can. Yet modern scientists insist that animals can't have feelings, and any inquiry into this question is ridiculed. There hasn't been a substantial formal inquiry into this question since Darwin wrote *The Expressions of Emotions in Man and Animals,*[14] over 120 years ago!

When it comes to ascribing emotions to animals or claiming the validity of intuition, science becomes silent and anecdotal data suddenly becomes unacceptable. This is particularly frustrating when contrasted with the fact that anecdotal data is used as validating proof in many scientific studies. In medicine, it is used whenever the observer has to rely on subjective responses rather than measurable data, as in studies of drugs used to treat pain. Pain is a completely subjective phenomenon. We can only infer that someone is in pain based on observed behavior or on the individual's statements. A patient's report of his or her level of pain would be considered an anecdote, which literally means "an unpublished story." Once these "stories" from patients are collected and published in the form of an article in a medical journal, they cease to be anecdotes and become case studies, carrying the full impact of scientific fact. With all the money spent on medical research, there must be millions of studies by now that involve reporting and tracking patients' symptoms, all of which are entirely based on the anecdotal evidence supplied by the patients about their level of discomfort. Such data — inferred, indirect, subjective data — carries no weight when applied to animals, nature, or the study of intuition.

There are probably many reasons for this resistance on the part of the scientific community, not the least of which is the fact that if animals and other life forms are seen as able to feel intensely and as equal to humans, they will have to be treated accordingly. This would require a change in virtually every aspect of modern life, particularly the world of commerce. If we conceded that animals could feel terror, grief, pain, and depression, we would no longer be able to exploit them so ruthlessly in the laboratory or the factory farm.

Far from being unworthy of scientific study, the field of intuitive communication with animals and nature is a new science. It may be outside the box of what traditional scientists can accept or will investigate, but maverick scientists are finding it fascinating and quite promising.

ANIMALS AND INTUITION

Animals know what we humans have forgotten: Staying connected to your core or intuitive self can be a matter of life and death. This is never so evident as when an animal who is otherwise friendly and amiable takes a violent and unexplained dislike to someone. Usually it is later discovered that this person is untrustworthy in some regard.

Margot Lasher writes about this in her book, *And the Animals Will Teach You.*[15] She relates several instances in which her dog, Hogan, warned her of impending danger. In one incident, Hogan gave Lasher strong, obvious warning messages at the door, but she went ahead and invited a man into her home to discuss hiring him for some household repair projects. He was an acquaintance of a friend of Lasher's, and had been described as trustworthy. When he came into the house, Hogan, who would normally be excited to explore a new person, sat frozen at the end of the couch watching this man. Then Hogan came over to Lasher and pushed himself between her and the back of the couch, something he never did before nor since. At that point, Lasher finally understood and was able to get the man out of the house. She later found out that he was taking drugs and could not be trusted.

Rupert Sheldrake, a Ph.D. microbiologist, is one of the few biologists to turn his attention to the field of intuition.[16] He conducted a study, using statistical analysis and controlled experimental conditions, on the phenomenon of animals that know intuitively when their people are coming home. He repeatedly videotaped one little dog who had an uncanny ability to go sit by the door about ten minutes before his person appeared. All possible experimental bias was eliminated. The dog's person was sent out and given random instructions about when to return (sometimes she was to return immediately, other times she was to stay away all day, etc.). She would not know her instructions until she was well away from home. The dog was alone in the house with the video camera running. The woman was not providing any inadvertent environmental clues, such as the noise of a car engine, because she traveled on foot. Sheldrake found that the dog's ability to predict the woman's return was highly significant statistically (p< 0.000001). He even let one of his critics run the experiment; it again came out statistically significant. The dog was predicting his person's return through some undetermined method; Sheldrake speculates that the method was intuition.

In fact, animals are masters of intuition. No one told them that intuition was silly or make-believe. Animals do not have the cultural limitations that we do. They communicate intuitively all the time, among and between species. For them, using intuition is just an enhancement of the five senses. They rely on their intuition to inform them of danger and to help them size up people, animals, and situations. Intuitive ability is the explanation for how animals can predict events and unerringly assess the true motives of a human being. It explains animals' erratic behavior before earthquakes and the assistance dog's ability to predict his person's seizures. When you work with animals to learn how to communicate, as you will be doing in this book, you will be working with the best teachers of intuition on the planet.

EXERCISES: BUILDING YOUR INTUITIVE SKILL

Here are three exercises you can use to develop your intuitive skill. Before you begin the exercises, find a notebook that you can use for all the exercises in this book. It should be of a reasonable size and tough enough to bring along on walks and on any field trips you might take to visit and speak with animals. Use this notebook to record your results for the exercises at the end of each chapter. Make sure to put a check mark or some other notation next to all your correct data. That way you can look back at your successes and have a quick way to assess your accuracy. You need this kind of feedback system to help you progress.

Exercise 1: Who's Calling?

Try to guess who is on the phone before you pick it up. Write down what you guess and keep a record. You should become pretty accurate within about two weeks of practicing this. At that point, you can try answering the phone by saying the person's name.

Exercise 2: Make Your Best Guess

Begin to build your intuition by consciously guessing the outcome of any unknown situation that confronts you in your daily life. Record your intuitive guesses about any undecided situation that arises: sports competitions, the success of some endeavor, or how bad the traffic will be.

Exercise 3: Record Your Hunches

Take your notebook with you throughout the day and record any random hunches, thoughts about the future, musings about why something is happening, or any other such intuitive information. You can ask yourself this question about any puzzling or confusing situation: "What does my intuition — my gut feeling — have to say about this?" Then record your answers. Read back through your notes after a week to see how accurate your intuitive musings were.

Chapter Three

Using Your Intuition to Communicate Nonverbally

I ntuitive communication is the universal language of all life; it needs no translation. Using intuition, I can mentally send words in English to a horse in Germany who has never heard English and be understood perfectly. As a universal language, intuitive communication has many intriguing features not present in spoken language. For example, it is instantaneous; huge banks of information can be transmitted in a nanosecond. When this happens, which is not all the time, the information comes as a sensation of knowing. You just somehow know in your mind everything about an animal's past or what is wrong with the animal. You know it all at once, as though the information were tossed to you all rolled up in a ball.

I compare spoken language to a typewriter and intuitive communication to the most powerful computer known. Unlike spoken language, intuitive communication can occur irrespective of time or space. This is what the scientists who study intuitive abilities are postulating[1], which means you can do this kind of communication over long distances and even use your intuition to look into the future and to examine events in the past.

In my consultations, I usually work with people by telephone or e-mail, contacting animal clients at a distance all over the world. Once when I was on a TV show in Europe, an animal behaviorist — brought on the show to challenge me — asserted that I simply read body language and made educated guesses based on my knowledge of animals. I countered by telling him that I rarely see my clients in person and I usually don't even look at a photograph of the animal. I just get the animal's name, age, and description, and then I tune in to the animal by closing my eyes and imagining what the animal looks like, as if I am seeing it on a big screen in front of me. This process feels a little like tuning in to a radio station. People ask me how I know I am getting the right long-haired black cat named Blackie, for instance. My response is that my intention to speak to that particular cat who belongs to the person who contacted me and who lives in the region described to me is what ensures the connection.

The connection I make is mental and emotional. In essence, I form an instantaneous relationship with the animal without ever seeing or meeting her and without the animal knowing me except through our intuitive exchange. Experience has shown me that it is not necessary to interact in person with an animal in order to form an intuitive connection. I can attest that the intuitively formed bond can be just as strong as any bond I have with one of my own animals.

In my work with animals, I try hard to avoid making educated or logical guesses, relying instead on information my intuition brings in. Often, what I receive is something illogical that I could not or would not have made up. That kind of information is almost guaranteed to have come from the animal.

For example, I was asked to communicate with a dog who was dying and find out what he wanted to do before he went. When I contacted the dog, he sent me pictures of a field with airplanes. I thought they were toy airplanes. He just kept showing me airplanes taking off and landing and said that was what he wanted to do. To me this made no sense. I know of no animals who like airplanes, and my instinct is to keep animals as far away from planes as possible. So I knew this was not something I would have made up. The dog was on the East Coast of the United States; I live on the West Coast. There were no clues I could have picked up by being in the dog's home. The woman had told me nothing about what the dog liked. When I described my results to her, she told me that her brother was a pilot who took the dog flying all the time, an activity that the dog loved.

To illustrate the physicists' speculation that this kind of perception can be used to examine the past, I will tell you about a case in which I interviewed an animal who had already died. I actually do this quite often, and I find it helpful for people who are having a hard time with grief and the process of letting go. When I work with an animal who has died, I contact the spirit of the animal using a description or working from a photograph to make the connection intuitively.

In this case, the animal was a cat who told me two peculiar things. First, he said his person made him laugh the week he was dying because she was carrying water around with her everywhere. Then he told me that the person's mother was very sick at the same time when he was dying. When I conveyed this information to the woman, she was confused. She could not imagine what it meant, and we both concluded that my results must have been "off." Then, about a week later, she called and told me that she'd realized I was right after all. During the last week of the cat's life, the woman had sprained her ankle and was carrying ice packs around (which the cat conveyed to me as water) in order to ice her ankle. Also around that time, her mother, who lived on another continent, had called to talk about an upcoming root canal procedure she was going to have.

A final feature of intuitive communication that sets it apart from spoken language is the fact that you don't have to deal with the problem of interference. When speaking out loud you have to be careful not to interrupt, and you can't have too many people talking at once or no one will be able to hear. But because intuitive communication is so fast, interference is not a problem. I have had thirty students ask the same questions at the same time to the same animal with no problems. Everyone got answers from the animal, and often they got the same verifiable answers. The only limitation I've observed occurs when the animal being questioned is uncomfortable with or afraid of people, in which case the animal will either voice her discomfort or just shut down and not say anything to anyone.

I can just about guarantee that you and your animals are exchanging information intuitively all the time. In his research on animals and intuition, Rupert Sheldrake[2] came across an amusing phenomenon that indicates that, while we may not be so good at hearing them, at least the animals are definitely hearing us. He heard from many people who told him that when it came time to go to the vet their cats would suddenly disappear. Sheldrake talked to some veterinarians about this and found one clinic that doesn't even make appointments for cats. That clinic just advises people to grab the cat and come in.

You may think it was your idea to get up and open the door for your animal or go fill that empty water bowl, but chances are you did it because you unconsciously received your animal's intuitive request for those actions. One day when I was sitting at my computer typing, my dog Brydie came by and nudged my elbow as she usually does (which is always so helpful for accurate typing). Typically I say hello and tell her, "Not now, I'm busy." But on that day I found myself immediately rising from my chair. In my mind, I had the thought that an animal had gotten out. Then I got the thought that I had to go to the front door. This was all coming from Brydie. When I got to the front door, it was open and one of the dogs had gotten out and was quite a few blocks away. Brydie may well have saved the dog from getting injured by coming to tell me about the problem. It's a good thing I was able to hear her and didn't just tell her to go away.

SENDING INFORMATION

Like all forms of communication, intuitive communication is two-way; you can both send and receive information. When two people are very close, they sometimes have the experience of being able to "read" each other's minds. This is an example of intuitive communication between humans. Since animals are experts at intuitive communication, just about any thought or feeling you send to an animal will be received. However, this does not mean that what you send will be immediately acted upon. If you are having a problem with an animal, you can't use this skill to control; you can only use it to negotiate and work toward improving your relationship.

The four main ways of sending information intuitively are:

1. Talking Out Loud: In this method you say what you want to communicate to an animal out loud in a normal tone of voice, using your normal vocabulary. The animal will receive it. It is important that you have the belief and the intention that what you are saying is being received. Even if you are skeptical about whether your animal can understand you, try suspending your judgment and do this as an experiment to see what happens. This technique of talking out loud can be used at a distance, too. If you are on vacation and want to communicate with your animals at home, you can talk out loud to them and the animals will hear you intuitively. The hotel staff might also hear you, so you may want to choose one of the other methods that follow for sending.

2. Thinking Your Message: There is really no difference between saying what you want to communicate out loud and thinking it. Thinking a message or question is useful when you have a crowd of people doing intuitive communication; otherwise things get too noisy. This method can also come in handy when you want to avoid appearing to be crazy for talking to your horse out loud while you are visiting him at the stable. It is useful any time you are restricted from making noise, such as when showing animals. Thinking your message is generally faster and easier than talking out loud, but it does take additional focus and concentration. It helps to close your eyes to block out distractions when you do this. You then hold the internal intention that your thoughts will travel where you send them and will be understood.

3. Sending a Picture: This method usually involves closing your eyes and making a mental picture or image of something, which you then send to the animal. Again, you have the intention that what you send mentally will reach its mark. You can do all your intuitive communicating this way if you wish. I like to use pictures specifically to show an animal what I want. For example, I might send a picture — almost like a movie — showing an animal how I want her to behave toward another animal. You can also send an animal a picture as a way to ask a question. For example, you might send a dog a mental image of a creek and ask her — by sending a thought mentally — if she would like to go in it. Then you watch the image, again like a movie, to see what the dog does.

4. Sending a Feeling: To use this method, you would concentrate on a specific emotion and then mentally send it to the animal with the intention of it reaching her. I use this method when I want to calm or comfort an animal. It is also a great way to send love to your animals when you have to be apart from them.

Here's a way to picture how these techniques work: whatever message you send intuitively, in whatever form, goes into an invisible translator box, metaphorically speaking, and then emerges in a form intelligible to the other party. It does not matter which method you use for sending information intuitively, the animal will just receive it in the form that is best for her. Intuitive communication is independent of distance; you can send information whether you are close or far away from whomever you wish to contact.

EXERCISES: SENDING INFORMATION INTUITIVELY

Try these exercises to explore what it feels like to send information to an animal. Do each exercise twice. The first time, do the exercise with an animal that is right there with you. Then do it a second time with an animal that is in some other location, perhaps an animal who belongs to a friend or relative. As you experiment with sending information using the four methods, remember to hold the intention that what you are sending is being received.

Exercise 1: Let's Talk

Practice talking to an animal out loud. Tell her something that you would like her to do for you.

Exercise 2: Mental Messages

Think of some qualities you admire in the animal. Now mentally send to the animal the thought that you admire those qualities. Your mental statement might be something like, "I admire your intelligence and beauty." Close your eyes and imagine that thought traveling through the air to the animal and being received.

Exercise 3: See This?

Send the animal an image of an object that you know or suspect she likes, like a particular treat or toy. Close your eyes and imagine this object. Then picture that image traveling through the air to the animal, as you did in Exercise 2. Now imagine the animal being able to see the image you sent.

Exercise 4: Heart-to-Heart

Send a feeling of love to the animal. Close your eyes and imagine a feeling of love in your heart. Send the feeling through the air from your heart to the heart of the animal. Imagine that feeling being received by the animal.

Don't be surprised if you get some strange results with these exercises. Your animals are hearing you. When you send an image of her favorite toy to your dog, she might just run to get it. When you send love to your cat, she might come curl up in your lap. The animals are responding to your communicating with them.

I once did this exercise with my horse, who was emotionally shut down when I got him and did not know how to be affectionate. "I wish you would give me a kiss like other horses do," I said to him. Then I visualized his giving me a kiss. At that point, he craned his neck over the fence and gave me the biggest, sloppiest horse kiss I've ever gotten. It just about cured me from asking him for a kiss again!

RECEIVING INFORMATION

Information can be received intuitively in any of five modes: hearing, feeling, seeing/knowing, smelling, or tasting. None of them is better than the other, nor are they mutually exclusive. When I started doing intuitive communication, I received information primarily as words and pictures. Most people start out being better at receiving in one or two of the modes than the others, but which modes are strongest varies from person to person. You may find that you only get intuitive information as feelings at first, and it can be a bit frustrating. But as you practice, you will quickly develop the ability to receive easily in all the modes. Which mode you use will become less important once you become more skilled; the information will just come to you in a variety of modes. You will be more focused on *what* you are getting rather than on *how* the information is coming in. For each of the different modes below I am including a story — either one of mine or one from a student, client, or colleague — to illustrate how the mode works. Later, you will practice receiving in each mode through focused exercises. For now, I just want to introduce you to the concepts.

Hearing

Some people are able to hear words and phrases intuitively right away, and some find it the most difficult mode. Everyone is different. Hearing can be a hard mode to master because the words you hear usually sound like your own voice. Therefore, the tendency is to assume that you are making things up. The only way around this is to do verifiable exercises so you can't deny the accuracy of your results or the fact that they came from outside of yourself. When you hear an animal intuitively, you may get single words or whole phrases. Once you get good at it, the experience is like taking dictation.

My favorite story about intuitively hearing an animal talk comes from a colleague of mine, Janet Shepherd. When Janet was learning to do intuitive communication, a friend asked her to take care of her horse. Janet went over to meet the horse and get instructions for its care. As the woman was explaining things, in her head Janet distinctly heard the words, "Cows are...." She looked around and no one was there but her friend and the horse. Then she heard the word "ugly." Immediately after that, her friend said, "Oh, by the way, don't take the horse up on the hill; there are cows up there, and this horse hates cows."

Mari Anoran, one of my students, sent me the following story of her experience with hearing an animal speak to her. This incident occurred before she started taking classes in intuitive communication:

One Indian Summer afternoon, my life changed suddenly but wonderfully. My husband, Dan, and I were driving through a shopping area when we saw a shelter rescue organization with their adoption animals in makeshift cages on the sidewalk. We had been interested in getting a dog for some time, so we decided to take a look. Dan went to play with the puppies while I, being a practical person, went to check out the older dogs. I considered a quiet golden retriever mix, but didn't feel a connection. I turned to speak to Dan, and then...I saw him: a handsome, black-and-white puppy with big, brown, soulful eyes. I knelt down and looked into his face as he pressed his muzzle against the wire mesh that separated us. The thought, "I'm the one!" flashed in my mind. Without thinking, I turned to Dan and said, "He's the one." Dan grimaced, "Him? Why him?"

"He's the one," I insisted.

Meanwhile, "the one" was lying passively while the other puppies barked and wriggled. Dan was not impressed; he wanted a manly, alpha dog. Nevertheless, at my urging he approached the rescue staff. I was sure we'd be more than acceptable parents, but as the woman ticked off the requirements — house with yard (no), home during the day (no) — my confidence ebbed. We were summarily rejected. Feeling chastened, we tried to do our shopping but could not get the dog off our minds.

Dan could tell how upset I was. "Let's go back and try again," he said. This time, another staff person was on duty and cheerfully agreed to consider us. However, he said that another couple had already adopted the dog and that there were five couples on a waiting list for him! We were stunned. Still, I insisted we put our names down. We left our cell phone number and begged the woman to call if anything changed. Despite the futility, I began to feel oddly hopeful.

We continued shopping, and about an hour later we got a call on the cell phone. Dan answered immediately and I heard the excitement in his voice. He hung up grinning and said, "We got him." We rushed back to claim our boy, whom we named Kersey. The staff person explained that the couple who'd originally adopted Kersey changed their minds and the shelter wanted us to have him. After I filled out the paperwork, Dan knelt down and Kersey leaped into his arms and into our lives, changing us forever.

Feeling

This mode of receiving intuitively is probably the easiest for most people, especially when they are starting out. When information comes in intuitively as a feeling, you will get a sense of something or a feeling about something. For example, you might ask a dog you don't know whether she likes children. In response, you might get a vague negative feeling, or you might feel cold, or you might experience a flash of anger. Any of those feelings would be informing you that the dog probably doesn't like children.

You can also receive physical feelings in this mode. Let's say you

ask a horse whether she has any muscle stiffness, and then you immediately feel a pain in your low back. When you investigate, you may
well find that the horse has some pain in that same region of her
body. When I teach people to interview animals about physical well-
being, I encourage them to learn how to assess physical feelings at a
distance without taking those phantom sensations into their body; it
is much more pleasant that way. If you tend to take on the physical
symptoms of others because you are highly empathic, there are techniques you can use to clear this energy out of your body.[3] You can
train yourself not to take on others' energy, and you will still be effective at using intuition to help a sick or injured animal. This subject
is covered in more detail in chapter 12.

Another student, Star Dewar, sent me these stories about how
she used her intuition to find some lost dogs. You will see that she
was mostly working in a feeling mode. She writes:

One day the fattest, most adorable dog showed up at my
house early in the morning, out of breath. Well, of course
she was out of breath; this girl dog was part pit bull and
part potbellied pig! All fifty pounds of her crawled up into
my lap and wanted to lick my face. I knew she was lost,
and I asked the angels to help me find her home. The
plain and simple answer they threw back at me was, "Well,
you know animal communication; just put her in the car
and take her home!" Oh, fine. So I put her in the car and
went down the hill to the highway. I asked her, "Okay, do
you live to the right or left?" I got a definite nudge to the
right, so I turned right. I continued to the right down
the highway, then I noticed her staring at a house. "Do
you live there?" I asked. I got a "no" feeling. "But you
know this house, right?" I asked. I got a feeling like, "yes."

So I turned down the little lane where that house was. Then she began staring at another house farther down the lane. I asked her the same two questions and this time I heard her say, "Yes, I know this house." I stopped and a dear elderly man walked out. "Sorry to bother you, sir, but do you know this dog?" My heart sang when he said, "Yes, I know who she belongs to; she used to come visit me often! I will run in and get the phone number." So that is how I got her home. It turned out that she lived behind the first house she had been staring at.

I had a second incident soon after this. Our dog Holler Hound, a former hunting dog, took off in the hills near our house. I went down the road a little and tuned into her. I sensed that she did not want to come home and that she was having a ball running all over the place. I faced toward the east and asked her if she was in that direction, and got a feeling of "no." I kept on changing direction until I got a "yes" feeling, then I started walking and calling her. About two minutes later, I could hear the tinkle of her tags and the crunching of her paws on the dry leaves. I mentally asked her to come to me, and I felt it right away when she relented and started running in my direction. Then I saw her, and she came right up to me. It took some convincing, but it worked. I could have walked all over the place, and who knows how long she would have dragged out her expedition or where she might have surfaced?

Seeing/Knowing

Seeing and knowing are both aspects of the same mode; both involve clairvoyance, or "clear seeing." When you receive in the seeing aspect of the mode, you may find it easier to work with your eyes closed. The pictures you receive intuitively may be like individual still photographs, or they may be like scenes from a movie. Usually they convey a lot of information in a few simple images.

For example, a woman called to ask me to figure out why her horse did so poorly at shows. When I talked with the horse, I couldn't find anything really wrong. The horse seemed pretty happy and did not seem uncomfortable. But throughout our conversation, I kept getting an image of a gray cat. When the woman called back, I told her that I just couldn't figure out what was wrong. Then I asked her if she had any idea why I kept seeing an image of a gray cat. "Oh yes," she replied, "that cat and my horse are inseparable. The cat and the horse eat together and sleep together. They are in love. Come to think of it, the only time they are apart is when the horse goes to the shows." Bingo.

In another example, a woman wanted me to ask her horse how he liked his new stable. The horse sent me a picture of a huge green pasture and a white barn. Then he told me that he "liked the old place better." The woman confirmed that the image I described corresponded to his old stable.

When intuitive information comes in through knowing, you just know it. You don't know why or where it came from, it just pops into your head. It can sometimes be a bit disconcerting.

I have the experience of knowing quite often during my work. In a recent instance, a client called to find out why her horse was not doing well in dressage training. When I tuned in to the horse, the situation came to me all at once. I "knew" what the problem was and found myself jotting down an extensive narrative of the situation. In this "knowing" mode, it was as if I knew the horse quite well and could easily describe his feelings and what was going on with his life. The main problem I identified was his trainer, who I believed was being negative about the horse. I was convinced this trainer was telling the woman to get rid of her horse, that the horse was "not good dressage material," and that he would "never amount to much." Of course, I had only my intuitive "knowing" to go on; I had no proof as yet. But when I reported back to the woman with my findings, she confirmed everything. She said the trainer was being negative and telling her all the things I had identified.

My client was trying to ignore what was happening, but it was not so easy for the horse to ignore it — hence his bad behavior. Logically, poor performance in a horse can be caused by any number of factors: an ill-fitting saddle, an uncomfortable bit, pain from a past injury, illness, or abuse by a person. Unkind trainers are just one possible cause, but my intuition helped me identify it as the exact cause in this case. My client was grateful to discover the problem. Since she had no intention of getting rid of her horse, she found a new trainer who appreciates her horse, and she and her horse are now doing well in their lessons. This story also illustrates the fact that animals really do hear and react to thoughts and words directed their way.

Smelling and Tasting

Obviously these are two distinct modes, but I'm combining them in one category because they are similar to one another and because the rare person who primarily receives information via smells usually also receives impressions of tastes (and vice versa).

I often get intuitive impressions of smells and tastes when I work with lost animals because I specifically ask questions about these senses: "What smells have you encountered? What does it smell like where you are now? What have you eaten? What did it taste like?" I asked a cat who had escaped from his New York City apartment to tell me what he could smell in his current location. The response I got was "something fishy." It turned out that he was trapped in the basement of the Chinese restaurant next door.

In a recent class, I had the students question each others' animals to find out the animals' favorite foods. Often, such information will come through intuitively as sensations of taste or smell. When one student asked an unfamiliar horse this question, she received an impression of the taste of pears. Pears turned out to be on the top of the treat list for that horse.

Mode of Preference

As you do the exercises in later chapters, you will probably find that you have a favorite mode for receiving; mine is hearing. When I am working on a case and I get stuck, I ask the animal to tell me in words what is wrong. Sometimes, in response, I intuitively hear the animal say a word or phrase three times. When I get information that way, it almost always turns out to be accurate. Whatever mode of reception you end up liking best, just be aware that you can ask to have information sent to you intuitively in any mode you choose. In the chapters that follow, I will explain how to do that.

Chapter Four

Accuracy and
Verification

Accuracy is always of concern in intuitive communication. But how do you verify that the information you are receiving is correct? Sometimes you can get confirmation from the animal's person. Sometimes you might see a dramatic shift in an animal's behavior following your communication. But until you can actually check your data, your only real choice is to go with what you get — even if it seems illogical. This can often be challenging, as it was in the case of Red, a seventeen-year-old quarter horse belonging to Susan Whalton.

Susan called me because Red's behavior upon being bridled and ridden was getting progressively worse. He was so head-shy that she had to take the bridle apart to put it on him. He had begun whirling and spooking under saddle and was no longer safe to ride. Recently, Red had pulled back while tied and been injured. People were advising Susan to tie him to a post for a few days to teach him not to be head-shy, or to use tie-downs and harsh bits to hold his head down. She did not want to use these severe techniques.

Susan read about me in an article in the *Whole Horse Journal*,[1] and called as a last resort. She had already had two veterinarians examine Red, and they could find nothing physically wrong. The pressure was on for me to discover the emotional problems leading to his bad behavior. However, when I talked intuitively to Red, he distinctly told me that his problem was physical, not emotional. He said that he had a huge pain in his head and neck and that there was something really wrong with his teeth, maybe an infection. He wanted me to tell Susan that he was sorry about his behavior, but that his mouth hurt and he could not tolerate the bit. He wanted to be able to go riding with Susan, but as soon as the bridle went on he felt almost unbearable pain.

I knew that everyone thought Red had emotional problems, but I had to honor the information I received from him and relay it to Susan. I had no clue whether I was accurate or not. I suggested that Susan call an equine bodyworker to assess Red's head and neck, and gave her a referral to a friend, Lorinda Doxey, who is a certified equine trigger-point myotherapist. When Lorinda examined Red, she said the top of his head and neck were rock hard — the worst she had ever seen. He had practically no range of motion, and his lymph nodes were completely swollen. She felt he was probably in extreme pain.

Lorinda worked on Red for four days, and gradually enabled him to relax his muscles and regain some flexibility. She suspected that problems with his teeth were causing his tension, and suggested that Susan call an equine dentist to check Red's teeth. The dentist discovered that three of Red's lower molars had been ground into a mass by his upper teeth, a condition that would have caused him extreme pain. Once the problems with Red's head, neck, and teeth were addressed, he was able to return to riding and could tolerate bridling.

I now recognize that when a previously well-behaved horse starts to refuse to bridle, has high head carriage, and becomes dangerous to ride, problems with the teeth are a likely cause. Consequently, when someone calls with that collection of complaints, I advise them to spend their money on an equine dentist and a good equine bodyworker first, to rule out physical pain as a cause.

HOW ACCURATE IS IT?

I find that when someone calls about a lame horse I am usually able, without seeing the horse, to identify the leg the horse is favoring. Also, I can often determine the location of a caller's lost animal. This success comes from years of practicing and refining my intuitive communication skills, and it is no longer surprising to me. I can't imagine, though, ever losing the thrill of being able to do something that seems impossible — and that often proves so helpful for people and their animals.

However, while intuition can be highly accurate, it is not infallible. Intuitive assessment is a skill that you must practice. When you start out, your accuracy is guaranteed to fluctuate. Even now, I can sometimes be inaccurate or even completely off, and I make sure to warn people of that. I tell my clients that they need to be the final judge of whether the information I give them proves correct.

No reputable intuitive I know of, working with people or animals, claims to be totally accurate. Typically, they claim an accuracy rate of about 80 to 90 percent. I believe my accuracy rate for most cases is about that, too, but those are rough estimates, not systematic ones. I know that my accuracy rate goes down with lost animals — in part because the animal is upset and his situation may be constantly changing.

I realize that it's hard to believe that intuitive communication can be accurate. Skepticism is to be expected when you are first introduced to this field. You will only be able to believe it once you have undeniable proof. To obtain that for yourself, you will have to do repeated, verifiable exercises.

ANECDOTAL EVIDENCE

Most of the information that supports the accuracy of intuitive communication is anecdotal. Because this work is not being done in controlled laboratory experiments, it tends to be rejected as invalid by the scientific community. While it would be great to design and carry out a controlled experiment to statistically test the validity of intuitive communication with animals, I doubt that confirmed skeptics would credit even statistically significant data. Certainly, Sheldrake's statistical study of the dog who could predict his person's return[2] has not had the reception it deserves in scientific circles.

Here is an example of what I mean by anecdotal evidence. During an advanced class, I asked a student, Renee Gallegos, to talk with my cat Hazel and inquire about Hazel's life before she came to live with me. When Renee contacted Hazel, these were her impressions:

I see a run-down area near water. There is a café nearby. It feels like Hazel is alone, like she was dumped here. She has to find her own food. There are boats. I see her coming directly toward you with her tail up. She knows she is going to go home with you. I see some drums, big drums, big gray drums. Why am I seeing drums? Why am I getting the word "toxic"?

At that point, Renee opened her eyes and wanted to know what I knew about Hazel's past. I told her that I met Hazel while on a job at a houseboat dock in the Port of Oakland in California. I was sent to clean up a batch of unidentified fifty-five-gallon drums (some of which were gray) that were suspected of containing toxic materials. As I arrived, Hazel walked right up to me from the middle of those drums, meowing, with her tail in the air. When I saw her, I said to myself, "I want that cat!" The facts were: Hazel was a stray, she was scrounging for food, and there was a café near the boat dock.

SKEPTIC'S CLAIMS

What I find astounding is that committed skeptics would come up with some excuse for debunking such evidence. They would not accept that the details of this case prove that Hazel and Renee were exchanging information mentally. Such skeptics would say that Renee probably asked me subtle but leading questions to obtain a correct answer. But Renee didn't ask me any questions; she just talked to Hazel and reported her intuitive impressions.

Setting aside the idea that Renee was "cold reading" — subtly pumping me for the right answers — skeptics might charge that she was using logic and making lucky guesses based on past experience and education. However, I told Renee only that Hazel was a rescued cat. Using logic, Renee might have guessed that I got Hazel from an animal shelter because the majority of rescued cats come from a shelter or are given away in front of a supermarket. There is no way that Renee could have gotten all the information she did by making educated guesses. So what other sleight of hand could she have used? My contention, of course, is that there was no chicanery and no lucky guessing. Renee spoke with Hazel, and Hazel spoke with Renee. That's it.

UNDENIABLY ACCURATE

In my mind, subjective, anecdotal evidence is quite good enough to support the validity of intuitive communication. Read the following cases and see if you don't agree.

In one of my practice groups in animal communication, I asked the students to contact my horse, Dylan, using just a photograph of him. They had not seen him in person or visited his stable. I suggested that they ask him various questions, one of which was, "How do you feel about cats?" Only one of the students knew anything about horses, so the rest of them had no basis for making an educated guess in response to this question. It turned out that they all got exactly the same information, but they were hesitant to reveal their results because they all thought their answers were silly and wrong. What Dylan told them was that he was worried about stepping on cats and that he did not like it at all when cats jumped on his back. Only Dylan and I knew that there was a cat at his stable who loved horses, would walk all around their feet, and liked to jump on their backs if she got the chance. In fact, she had just jumped on Dylan's back earlier that week. Someone who knows horses and cats might suspect that something like that could happen, but it is certainly not typical barn-cat behavior. It is not something anyone would have logically surmised, least of all those students.

During an individual training session I conducted for a woman, we worked with Dylan again, this time in person. I told her the name of Dylan's trainer, Tina, and asked her to find out how Dylan felt about Tina. The student closed her eyes, connected with Dylan, then opened her eyes again and said, "There are two Tinas. He's telling me there are two trainers named Tina. One is tall and one is short. Why am I getting two Tinas? What is going on?" The student was absolutely right. I had forgotten that Dylan had a previous trainer who was also named Tina. The student was right about their looks too; one of the Tinas is tall and the other is of medium height.

Here is another example. I was called by a woman in Delaware about her dog, Zack, who had wandered off during a walk and become lost. When I contacted him intuitively (from California), he showed me that he was alive but unable to move and stuck in some shallow water. Then a complete scene unfolded in my mind's eye. I saw Zack sitting in water at the base of a long, gradual slope. I could see two hand-built stone walls that joined right behind him. Mentally, I stepped back and upward from the scene and was able to see which way the woman had to travel from her house in order to reach this point on the stone wall. When she called, I gave her the information. She said she knew the area I was describing, but had already looked there. I suggested she check the area again. She did so, and at the urging of a friend, she went just a little farther down the slope than before — just far enough to see Zack sitting in shallow water near the stone walls.

As far as I remember, I've never been to Delaware. I certainly did not check a satellite photo of the woman's town or call someone in Delaware to do some quick reconnaissance for me so that I could say something that sounded plausible to this woman. There is no way that I could have logically constructed the information that I received intuitively. Zack actually showed me where he was, and his person was thus able to save him and get him home.

SOMETIMES THE PROOF IS IN THE OUTCOME

When you work intuitively with an animal regarding a behavior problem, the proof of accuracy may come in the form of improved behavior. This was the case with Norman, a basset hound who moved into my town. Norman was not happy about the move and he was driving his people crazy by howling at all hours, practically nonstop. This had been going on for about three weeks. His people were becoming sleep-deprived and desperate. They loved Norman, but they did not know what to do. A neighbor suggested they contact me.

Because he lived down the street from me, I went to Norman's house and ended up working with him in person for about three hours, doing bodywork, listening to him, and negotiating. What I pieced together from Norman and his people was that Norman had moved from a place where he had enjoyed total freedom. At his old residence, in the wilds of northern California, Norman would leave in the morning, traverse a huge territory doing many interesting and important things, and return at night to the comfort of home. He had the life. Then he got moved into town, in a house with a postage-stamp yard. He was miserable.

What Norman and I did for most of the session was negotiate. I suggested things that might help make his life here more pleasant and he gave me his responses to my suggestions. He finally agreed to a series of jobs that he would do around his house for his people, and another batch of jobs that he would perform daily around town. The jobs would make him feel needed and would take the place of the self-appointed jobs he'd done in his previous home, such as roaming his territory and checking on the neighbors. One of his new jobs was to go with someone every day to check on the fire station and the post office and make sure everything was in order there. Also, his help would be enlisted in the home business that his person operated; he would give her moral support and help her think clearly and be more organized. I wrote all these jobs down and posted them on the refrigerator in Norman's house. His people were to remind him of his jobs, keep up their end of the deal, and praise him for doing his jobs so well. Norman also wanted to be assured that he could go back once each month to romp in his old neighborhood. From that day forward, the howling stopped and Norman became a happy, well-adjusted city dog.

In another behavior problem case, Beth Haylock called me about her dog, Sarah, who was being very aggressive toward guests and even relatives who came to visit. In my session with Sarah, I learned that she had been abused by her previous people and was unable to trust any humans other than Beth. I explained to Sarah that she could look into people's hearts to see if she could trust them. I also told her that Beth would always warn her before a guest came to visit, and that Beth would tell Sarah all about the person, including whether the person appeared to be trustworthy. I told Sarah to just look up at Beth to find out whether the guest could be trusted, and Beth would tell her. Sarah underwent a remarkable change after that session. She stopped her aggressiveness, and could be seen continually looking up into Beth's eyes whenever a guest was around, seeking confirmation that the guest was safe. It actually took Beth a little while to recall the deal I had struck with Sarah; for a day or two, she kept wondering why Sarah was looking up at her so often.

WHY INACCURACIES HAPPEN

The main thing that gets in the way of accuracy is your brain — specifically, your cerebral cortex. This part of your brain functions almost as a police officer would, directing traffic in your life and trying to keep you on the straight and narrow. When you stray into something weird like animal communication, your cerebral cortex may panic and try to push you back into the world of logic and order. The dilemma is that in order to activate your intuition, you must to turn off your tendency to figure things out with logic and past experience. Typically, when beginning students ask questions of animals, they tend to dismiss illogical information, trying instead to produce logical answers. But what's required in intuitive communication is a total surrender to your stream of consciousness. The only role your mind should play is to recognize information as it comes in and see that it gets recorded.

The students who learned that Dylan did not want cats on his back did receive the information, but rather than recording it they immediately tried to suppress it because they thought they were wrong. The police in their cerebral cortex were saying, "That's weird. Don't say it out loud because you'll make a fool of yourself." This is a common response for beginning students. We have spent many years training ourselves to fit in, be normal, and use our logic in all situations. Intuitive communication asks you to do something completely at odds with these lifetime habits. It's hard to overcome years of conditioning; I still make errors sometimes when, unaware, I slip out of intuition and into logical analysis.

Another problem that reduces accuracy is getting too much prior knowledge about an animal from his person. When you know too much, it's hard to be a blank slate and just let information come in without preconception. That's why I caution my clients to tell me very little about their animals. With lost animals, I ask them not to tell me what they suspect happened or anything that anyone else has speculated.

Your physical well-being can also affect your ability to communicate intuitively. If you are at all tired when you close your eyes to connect with an animal, chances are you will start to nod off and drift into sleep. Your body is just being opportunistic and taking any available break to get the sleep it needs. So you have to be well-rested to attempt this. Serious illness, excessive use of alcohol or drugs, or a diet high in sugar and processed foods can make it difficult for you to concentrate and focus to the extent necessary to succeed at intuitive communication.

Contrary to what you might imagine, if you practice intuition regularly you actually get more grounded and more in touch with your body rather than becoming "spacey." Think of how grounded most animals are; they are masters at intuitive communication. I have found that intuitive communication puts you directly in touch with your body. If your body is not happy, that will probably be the strongest message you receive when you tune in to your intuition, until you do something to address your body's needs.

Changes in hormone levels can also affect your ability to connect intuitively. Medical intuitive Mona Lisa Schultz discusses this in detail in her book, *Awakening Intuition.*[3] She says that women become even more attuned to their intuition once they go through menopause.

Former military researcher Joe McMoneagle teaches "remote viewing" — the military term for intuitive communication. McMoneagle found that a certain time of day is maximally conducive to intuitive endeavors. According to him, some military researchers found that high accuracy in subjects correlated with the one-hour period before and after 13.5 hours Local Sidereal

Time, or solar time. Solar time runs on a twenty-four hour clock, but it is a few minutes behind our normal clock and varies according to latitude and longitude.4 They also observed that, when there were sunspots, the subjects in their studies evidenced diminished intuitive ability.5

Then again, sometimes you can be wrong for no discernible reason. Whether or not you can pinpoint the cause, you should treat the issue of inaccuracy gently. If you expect too much too soon or come down too hard on yourself, you will get discouraged and not want to continue learning. If you get an answer that doesn't make sense or appears to be wrong — even if someone emphatically tells you it's wrong — I advise you to reserve judgment. Resist feeling like a failure and beating yourself up for being stupid and inept. Instead, just say to yourself, "Hmmm. I wonder why that information came in." I give this advice because people may tell you that the information you received isn't correct, but it could just be that their memories are faulty. What you discovered may actually prove to be correct. Clients often call me back to tell me that my information about their animal was right after all.

I recall a student who became discouraged after a beginning class. She worked with a dog in the class who told her that he really loved his red bed, but when she talked to the dog's person to get verification, she was told that the dog did not have a red bed. The next day when the student came to class, she was treated to the sight of the dog's person entering with a red sleeping bag in hand, proclaiming that she had forgotten all about her dog's daytime bed: a red sleeping bag on the back porch.

BEYOND VERIFICATION

Some things fall outside the realm of verification; they simply can't be confirmed. If you talk with the spirit of an animal who has died, you may be able to verify some of what he tells you. For example, you can ask him about the details of his life before he died and get verification of those. But when you venture into the realm of the spirit, no one can act as an arbiter — and really it doesn't matter. The process can be so helpful for the living, left behind and surrounded by grief, that you will simply know internally when you have succeeded in being a conduit for the animal to connect with those he loved.

When you do the exercises at the end of the book — related to communicating with wildlife, plants, and the natural landscape — your opportunities to get confirmation of your results will diminish. That's why we will start out working with domesticated animals, asking questions for which the answers can be verified.

Part Two

Getting
Started

Chapter Five

A New Way
of Talking

There are two parts to intuitive communication with animals: talking and listening. I will begin by teaching you how to talk to animals intuitively. This is by far the easier of the two skills to learn, but it may require a shift from the way you talk to animals now. In the approach I'm suggesting, you assume that animals are as intelligent and as emotionally complex as you are. This can be a stretch even for confirmed animal lovers.

I talked to animals before I got involved in this field, but I was not aware of how well they could actually understand me. All of us have been taught to think of animals as limited when compared to humans, certainly in terms of their ability to understand us. Because of my experience with intuitive communication, I now believe that animals understand us perfectly when we talk to them; they also comprehend every thought and feeling we have toward them.

My favorite story about how animals actually do understand us comes from a Canadian newspaper article about a cat named Pierre.[1] Pierre had a peculiar habit of going around to all the neighbors and bringing clothing and sheets back home to his person. She, in turn, would wash the articles and put them in a basket on her back porch, informing her neighbors that if they were missing something they were welcome to check the basket. The neighbors took to leaving their dirty laundry outside for Pierre to fetch. Pierre's person said that she was spending a fortune in laundry soap. The biggest thing Pierre brought home was a set of flannel sheets that he dragged halfway up the driveway.

One day the woman's daughter came to visit. The two women were sitting in the living room with Pierre when the daughter remarked that she had forgotten to bring her jogging suit, and she was disappointed that she would not be able to go jogging. The mother turned to Pierre and said, "Pierre, did you hear that? Why don't you go get her a jogging suit?" They both laughed, and the daughter told Pierre that she wanted a maroon jogging suit if he could arrange it. The next morning, a maroon jogging suit was on the floor in the living room, in exactly the daughter's size.

TALKING AS IF THEY UNDERSTAND

The talking experiment I suggest you try — with your own or a friend's animal — is this: for the next two weeks, hold the belief that the animal perfectly understands everything you say out loud and everything you think or feel toward her. I realize that this requires a leap of faith, but just think of it as an experiment. If it doesn't feel right or doesn't work, you can always go back to your old way of relating. I suspect, though, that when you do this experiment you will find that the animal will begin to relate to you in quite a different manner, and you will become fascinated by the changes you see.

It is hard to imagine how it is possible for an animal to understand spoken language or to receive our thoughts and feelings. The translator box image that I mentioned in chapter 3, on page 35, is one way to conceive of this process. It is as if there is a translator box located somewhere between you and the animal you wish to contact. Whatever you say, think, or feel toward the animal goes into that translator box and comes out the other end in a form the animal can understand. It doesn't really matter what language you speak, whether the animal has ever heard the language you're using, or whether you simply send a feeling or a thought to the animal instead of saying something out loud. Everything you send will be transmitted to the animal because that is your intention, and it will then be translated into a form that the animal can comprehend. Some animal communicators assert that animals are limited in their intuitive abilities and can only send and receive information via images. In my experience, animals can send information intuitively with the same, if not more finesse as humans — using either words, feelings, ideas, or images.

I often suggest to my clients that they try this experiment of talking to animals as if the animals understand, and I've received hundreds of responses about how well it worked. Here are a few of them.

Deb Steinberg sent in this story about her mare, Star:

I have six horses and one of them WILL NOT TRAILER. She is an older quarter horse mare who is lame, and she refuses to load into a trailer. We recently bought new property and had to move our horses. I read your Web page about how to talk to animals, and I decided to try it on Star. I started talking to her about the move two weeks before the scheduled date. I told her that she could not stay behind; all her friends would be leaving and she would need to get in the trailer when the time came. I explained that it was too far to walk and that the new people who bought our place would not let her stay. I told her that I knew she was frightened by the trailer, but that I hoped she would decide to join us in the new place. I talked to her every few days after that, reminding her that the time was coming and that I hoped she would be brave and come with us. She actually looked as if she were listening to me.

So when the day finally came to move the horses, I decided to move Star and her best friend first. I loaded her friend, and then as I haltered Star I reminded her of our conversation and told her that this was the day. That old girl practically dragged ME to the trailer and then she hopped right in! After we unloaded her at the new place, she acted like she was proud to be the first one there. As I brought the other horses, Star was right at the fence to whinny to them that she had checked it all out and it was fine!

Gina Richards tried the talking technique one hot summer day with her cat Missy. She went into the bathroom where she found Missy resting in the tub and said to her, "Missy, it is such a hot day, I really think it would be more comfortable for you in the closet where it's cooler. Why don't you try it?" Gina was shocked when Missy pointedly got up, walked through the studio to the edge of the closet, stuck her nose in the closet as if to sniff and test the temperature, and then looked up at Gina as if to say, "No, I don't think so, Mom." Missy then turned right around and went back to her preferred bathtub retreat.

Suzanne Martin sent me this story about her horse named Paco:

The first couple of times I fed apple cider vinegar and garlic to Paco, I noticed that he did not eat all of his grain and that he didn't seem fond of the taste. The next day, after I had given him his grain, I noticed that he hadn't finished it and had walked away to go eat his hay. I was standing outside his stall looking down into his feed bucket, and then I looked at him. He turned to look at me and walked over to see what I was doing. (He was now standing over his feed bucket facing me.) I said, "Paco, you need to finish your grain. I know it may taste funny, but it has stuff in it that is really going to help you feel better. It's also going to help heal the sores on your ankles." Paco then looked down into his feed bucket, looked back at me, and proceeded to eat the remaining grain. At first I couldn't believe what I was seeing. After a couple of seconds of not knowing what to say, I told Paco that he was a good boy, and that this stuff really was going to help him feel better. I am happy to report that, from that day forward, he has eaten all of his funny-tasting grain and no longer leaves any in his feed bucket.

Petra Gout tried the technique with her enormous orange cat named Tom. Tom was acting very cheeky to the other cat in the house and generally being disagreeable. Petra got stern with him and explained that if he did not shape up she was going to adopt three additional cats and then he would have his hands full. After she made this pronouncement, Tom began to howl and moan in a most uncharacteristic way. He would not stop until Petra told him she was just kidding.

Communicating with your animal as if you are talking to an equal can be especially effective when you are dealing with a behavior problem. To do this, speak from your heart and explain everything you are feeling about the situation and the animal's behavior. You can talk out loud if that feels more comfortable, or you can close your eyes and just think or feel the messages you want to convey. Your animal will understand either way. Explain why you want the animal to change and describe your hopes and dreams for the future. Try to maintain a feeling of equality in the discussion; negotiate rather than giving an ultimatum. Offer some incentive — either a reward or some action on your part — that would encourage the animal to behave as you wish. When you learn in later chapters how to hear what your animal is saying, this process of negotiation can become a two-way conversation, but for now it will be one-way.

Once you have discussed all the issues, finish up with a segment in which you say to your animal, "This is what I would like to have happen." Then close your eyes and imagine scenes, as if in a movie, of the outcome you most desire. If visualizing is not your strong suit, just imagine the feeling of things working out the way you would like them to. Your animal will receive this template for the future, and will understand precisely what it is you want.

This talking technique, of course, is no substitute for a good, positive training program, and it won't magically turn your animals into well-behaved angels. But it can help shift things, sometimes quite dramatically.

That's what Myrna Krohn found when she tried this new way of talking with her warmblood gelding, Bear. He was not doing very well in his training practice sessions, and at the dressage shows he got so nervous that he always performed poorly and came in last. When I do intuitive consultations, I often give people advice about how to resolve unwanted behaviors and where to go to get professional help with their animals. For behavior problems, I take what I call the "kitchen sink" approach: I relay every potential course of action that comes to me intuitively during the conversation with the animal, as well as everything I can think of from similar cases that might prove helpful. When I talked with Bear, he complained of how boring dressage practice was. It also became clear as I talked with Bear that both he and Myrna had anxiety about competing. I suggested that Myrna talk to Bear during her practice sessions and tell him that if he did very well at something during practice, rather than make him do it over and over she would take him to see the donkeys, which he loved, or take him out on the trail for a bit. Myrna did this, and Bear's behavior in practice turned stellar almost overnight.

For the shows, I advised Myrna to dose Bear and herself with Rescue Remedy (a flower essence formulation[2] that has a calming effect), work to slow and deepen her breathing when riding, and continually remind Bear that if he tried his best and they had fun, that was all she cared about.

At their next show, she implemented this program. While saddling, she kept talking to Bear saying, "Don't be nervous, it's just a warm-up." She said that Bear walked out of the barn supple in his back, with his head low and his ears relaxed; he led the way for the other horses who were nervous. The warm-up went smoothly. She reassured Bear mentally and sent him the thought that if he did his best that would be good enough for her. None of his old bad habits from previous shows surfaced. By the end of the show, she and Bear had won two first places, one second place, and the high-point ribbon. As they exited the arena with their awards, they received a standing ovation from all their friends who knew of Bear's previous difficulty in showing. She said that Bear was beaming.

Myrna tries to listen to Bear now when things go wrong, and she tries to read the signals he is giving her so that she can change what he doesn't like. In her words, "I'm trying to make him feel like a partner instead of a slave. Now I can bring out the horse I always knew was in there."

ARE THEY LISTENING?

When I talk with animals intuitively, I almost always do it with my eyes closed, and the animal is usually not nearby. Therefore I have little awareness of how the animal is physically reacting to being spoken to in this way. But that is one of the first things people want to know when they call for a consultation. They ask, "Do I have to put my animal up to the phone? Should she be awake and alert? Did you talk to her at 8:00 this morning? Because at exactly 8:00 she stopped what she was doing and sat with her head cocked for twenty minutes."

In truth, I never worry about getting the animal's attention. The animal doesn't have to be right by the phone or sitting politely in front of me when we talk. Intuitive communication can even occur when the animal is asleep; it really is quite different from spoken language.

However, I can offer a few observations of how animals react when you engage them in intuitive communication. In my classes, most of the animals attending are dogs. Sometimes we will have a whole room full of dogs, and before I got smart and started screening dog participants a bit better, there could be a whole roomful of rowdy, barking, brawling dogs. But invariably, no matter how hyper the dogs, when the people in the room closed their eyes to begin an intuitive communication session, each dog in the room would almost immediately get calm and lie down, often closing his or her eyes as well.

I have done in-home consultations with groups of cats in which all the cats scattered when I arrived, but emerged again to sit in a row staring at me after I closed my eyes and began the session. I've found that horses tend to approach me, drop their heads, and close their eyes while we talk intuitively. In one case, I was sitting in a chair in a horse's pasture. As I spoke with her, she continued to graze. I had my eyes closed, and I opened them now and then to check on her when writing notes. At one point in our conversation, she brought up an issue that she said was "the most important thing she had to say." At that moment, I felt her mouth on my hand. I opened my eyes to find her staring intently into my face, as if to say, "Did you get that? It's the most important thing!"

TALKING FROM A DISTANCE

Intuitive communication can be done just as easily from a distance as in person. I work with people all over the world without ever meeting their animals. Most of the time, I work by telephone, receiving only a description of the animal, not even a photograph. For foreign clients, I work almost entirely by e-mail. Whether in person, by phone, or by e-mail, the results seem to be equally accurate. For instance, Elaine Ho e-mailed me from Hong Kong with some questions for her dog, Coffee. One thing she wanted to know was what Coffee liked and didn't like. He told me that he liked his herbs (medicines), sleeping in bed with his people, the bathtub, people's feet, going visiting, and his fruit treats. He didn't like getting old, painful teeth, cats, and rain. Elaine e-mailed back to say, "That's him! That's my Coffee!"

Being able to talk from a distance is useful for connecting with your animals if you have to be away from them, either when at work or when traveling. Some of my clients have found it to be an effective aid in combating separation anxiety, a common problem in dogs. In these cases, I advise that you talk to your animal before leaving the house. Tell her where you are going, why, how long you will be gone, and when you will return. Just speak normally, as if you were talking to a person.

I believe that animals can understand the concept of time as we do. So saying something like, "I will be gone for about six hours and back at about 5:00 tonight," works just fine. There is no need to explain where the sun is or how many moons will pass before your return! Then, while you're away, tune in mentally and emotionally to your animal as often as you like, sending her your love and an account of what you're doing. Also remind her when you will be back.

I always recommend that my clients investigate holistic veterinary care. In my experience, the combination of a natural diet and holistic care regime produces much happier, healthier, calmer animals. In severe cases of separation anxiety, I urge clients to get massages for their animals to help calm them, and to try flower essences and herbs, too. These techniques have proven successful in many cases. The resources section of the book gives information on how to locate a holistic veterinarian. When you plan to be away for a business trip or a vacation, explain the particulars of your trip to your animal well before your anticipated departure. Tell your animal why you are going and why she can't come along. Tell her your departure and return dates, and describe how she will be cared for in your absence. Then promise her that you will talk with her from a distance while you are away, and make sure to keep that promise.

TALKING WITH ANIMALS WHO HAVE DIED

I believe that you can communicate intuitively with the spirit of an animal after she has died, and I do this for clients all the time. However, in those cases I'm working with people who are convinced that animals have spirits, so they believe that what I am doing is real. If you don't believe it's possible to do this, you can just skip to the next section. There is no way I can prove to you that this is possible and you don't have to believe in it to be able to communicate with animals intuitively. If you believe in this concept, you can try it for yourself in the exercises that follow.

It is possible to talk to the spirit of an animal regardless of how much time has passed since the animal died. As we've already discussed, anything you say will be heard by the animal. Once you have some practice at hearing what animals are saying to you, your conversation with the spirit of an animal can become a two-way exchange.

EXERCISES: TALKING AS IF THEY UNDERSTAND

Here are the exercises I described in this chapter. Try them out at your own pace. Be sure to record your results in your notebook.

Exercise 1: Talking As Equals

For two weeks, try this experiment: talk to your animals as if they hear and understand everything you say out loud to them and everything you think or feel about them. Also, hold the belief that they are just as evolved and intelligent as you are, and that you are dealing with beings who are equal, although quite different from you. For this exercise, all you will do is record any changes you note in their behavior as a result of this experiment.

Exercise 2: Problem Solving

If you have a particular behavior problem with your animal, try approaching her using the talking and negotiating method. Find a time to sit quietly with your animal. Send love from your heart, even if the situation is making you angry. Try to leave your anger at the door, so to speak, so that you can start anew with your animal. Explain exactly how you feel about the situation, from your heart, as if you were talking to an equal human being. Tell the animal why you feel the way you do about the situation. Discuss what you are thinking of doing if the situation can't be resolved. Request the behavior that you would like to see, and offer some incentive to the animal for complying. Now close your eyes and imagine (in feelings and pictures) exactly what you would like to have happen. Tell your animal, "This is my dream for how things could be." End by sending love again. Do this at least once each week. If there is any improvement whatsoever in the animal's behavior, make a huge fuss — praise, treats, the works — and continue the experiment. Record your results in your notebook.

Exercise 3: Talking from a Distance

When you are away from your animal at work or on vacation, you can tune in to her intuitively at any time by sending her love and a quick mental greeting. You can also send her a reassuring thought about how you are doing and tell her your estimated time of return. If you are on extended travel, you may want to have a longer session in which you sit in a quiet area, close your eyes, and imagine or feel your animal right there in front of you. Say the animal's name and send love. Then you can either talk out loud or send thoughts about how you are doing and how long it will be until you get back. You can also tell her anything you want her to do while you are away and send her an image of everything going well at home. These sessions can be done daily if you wish, but should be done at least weekly.

Exercise 4: Talking with an Animal Who Has Died

You can do this exercise with any animal from your past who has died, even the cat you had when you were three years old. Sit in a quiet place by yourself, close your eyes, and imagine the animal; either feel or see her right there in front of you. Say the animal's name and send love to her. Now say whatever is in your heart and mind. If you felt guilty about something related to the animal, talk about that in detail. Ask her if she can forgive you and give you a sign of her forgiveness. If you are still grieving and can't get beyond the tears, tell her that and ask her to help you learn to be happy again. Say whatever it is that went unsaid, and ask her to let you know in some way that you have been heard.

Exercise 5: Ask for Some Help

If you are having problems with something in your life — a mean boss, a difficult project, a puny bank account — try asking your animal to help you resolve the problem or achieve your goals and desires. You may be surprised at the results. Do this in the spirit of experimentation and see what happens. When Petra Gout heard this idea she immediately went to her cat Tom and told him she was sick of apartment living and wanted a nice house in the country. Within a month, she and her husband fell in love with a house they happened upon while touring the countryside one weekend. They found themselves unable to resist buying the house, which wasn't something they had been planning for at all. We're not sure whether Tom had a hand in this coincidence. Perhaps he helped manifest Petra's dream the same way we would do it, by visualizing her in a cottage in the country and asking the universe to help make that happen.

Chapter Six

Basic Techniques for Receiving Information Intuitively

Most people can become skilled at intuitively sending information to animals with minimal instruction; it's the intuitive receiving part that takes some study and practice. Sometimes receiving happens spontaneously. Many people have told me stories of unexpectedly hearing animals talking to them. However, this experience tends to be inconsistent and difficult to control. For consistency, you have to work a little.

A friend, Ann Joly, sent this story about hearing her animal talk to her unexpectedly one day:

A few years ago, I decided I wanted to do some pet-assisted therapy. How cool would it be, I thought, if you were in a nursing home, to have someone come visit you with a soft, cozy pet? Since I had just such animals in the form of two cats, I thought I'd give it a try. Maxx was a huge black cat who was laid back and easygoing; he even liked to ride in the car. Cuja was a shy girl, but very soft and purry, who loved having her head scratched. The cats passed their temperament tests and we were matched up with a nearby nursing home.

We visited the nursing home once a week on Wednesday nights for less than an hour. Initially, Maxx and Cuja didn't seem overly concerned one way or another with the visits once they got over the insult of being pushed and pulled in and out of their carriers. However, as time went on they seemed to remember Wednesday nights and became harder and harder to find at the critical hour. I sort of guessed that this was not the fun thing for them that I had hoped. However, at this point we were about six months into our visits and definitely had our "regulars" who counted on seeing us. So I struggled with this: While I was doing a wonderful, selfless thing for the residents at the home, was I torturing my cats at the same time? If I stopped going, would that be just another disappointment in a long string of letdowns to lonely elders? If I kept going, would I torment my own animals even more?

It was Halloween. I dressed up like a black cat with a long black tail, whiskers, and ears. I carved a pumpkin for the residents, loaded Maxx into his carrier, and headed for the nursing home. When we arrived, I pulled Maxx out and settled him in my arms, and off we went down the hallway where we were greeted by our usual friends. Maxx was quiet and tolerant in my arms for about a quarter of an hour. We were just leaving Mr. Johnson in the TV room and heading down the hall to the Wells sisters when Maxx communicated something to me loud and clear. The unmistakable message was, "If you put me in front of one more little old lady's face, I will rip her skin to shreds."

There was no struggling, no hissing, not even a tail wag, and the communication took me quite by surprise. But he couldn't have told me any more clearly if he had yelled at me using human words. I turned on my heel, cat costume and all, went back to the lobby, put Maxx back in his carrier — and away we went. That was it: the end of my pet therapy visits.

Another friend, Patty Bratsberg, sent me this story of her experience with hearing dialogue from her cat, which totally changed her relationship with animals:

Weezy, my eight-year-old Abyssinian cat, shared my home with four other cats but rarely came inside, preferring her private hunts and haunts. She was an excellent hunter, often leaving select trophies on the doormat to mark her success. That's why it caught my attention when she began staying indoors and following me around, often sitting near my feet and staring fixedly at me. At first, I was flattered by her unexpected attention. Her nickname was "the Princess" because she was usually rather standoffish and regal. As her odd behavior continued, I made a point of noting her weight, eating, and eliminations. Everything was normal.

Finally, one morning when she was again watching me, I asked her what was wrong. I was beginning to feel uneasy about her attentiveness and spoke out of frustration and concern.

To my astonishment I heard a reply in my head, "My stomach's wrong!"

The words seemed to come from my own familiar inner voice, but the wording of the statement was decidedly not my own. It both startled and impressed me that this was not something I was likely to say or guess as the problem. As a licensed veterinary technician, my vocabulary and experience would have led me to an entirely different description and diagnosis.

The next day, I took Weezy to the clinic where I worked and asked the veterinarian to examine her. He found nothing remarkable and doubted that she had abdominal trouble based on her appetite and weight and the absence of any sign of vomiting. To be safe we took X-rays, which revealed nothing definitive.

My concern remained. The doctor offered to do an exploratory surgery to ease my mind, and I accepted. That afternoon, he opened her up. To our surprise, her stomach was entombed in cancer. It was amazing that she could still eat without vomiting. Just as amazing was the realization that she had communicated the problem to me directly and correctly, against the better judgment of both the veterinarian and me.

This experience opened a door between Weezy and me for the remaining weeks of her life. We spoke often, and we talked about things greater than dying cats and their grieving owners. At the end, we were both remarkably peaceful and reconciled with the process and outcome. She let me know when she was ready to "go home," and I let her go.

Since then, I've shared similar experiences with numerous animals, usually in times of crisis or when I had to make an important decision regarding the animal. In every case, the encounters served to soften and resolve the difficulties and leave behind a warm legacy of deepened companionship, understanding, and trust. It is clear to me that we humans are always in the company of great and patient teachers, be they animals, stones, trees, or even tiny spiders. Should we learn to listen to them, perhaps our lives and ways would be transformed and expanded beyond anything we now know.

RECEIVING INFORMATION INTUITIVELY

In this chapter, you will learn the basic techniques for receiving information intuitively. When receiving, you will use one or more of the following modes (review chapter 3 for a more in-depth description of these modes):

- Hearing: receiving words and phrases mentally (for most people, this will sound like your own voice)
- Feeling: getting an emotional or physical sense about something from the animal
- Seeing and knowing: seeing images with your eyes closed that suggest information, and suddenly knowing answers to questions that you ask an animal
- Tasting: getting an intuitive impression of a taste
- Smelling: getting an intuitive impression of a smell

Which Mode Should You Use?

Usually when people first attempt to receive information intuitively, their feeling or empathic sense is the best developed and most accessible. To receive information in this mode, you ask the animal a question, either silently or out loud. For example, you might ask an animal to tell you what things he likes. Then turn your attention inward. Notice and record any and all ideas, hunches, impressions, and feelings that come to you.

When you work in the feeling mode, you can receive distinct feelings that are undeniably being experienced by the animals. I remember working with Linda Huck's rescued horse, Bo. Almost as soon as I connected with him I felt really sad, like I wanted to cry. As he and I talked, I learned about the abuse he had previously suffered. I worked with him to resolve some of his distress. Later, Linda related that she, too, felt sad and sometimes even cried when she was around Bo, but had not known the reason.

As a beginner, my strongest modes for receiving information turned out to be intuitive hearing and seeing. I discovered this by paying close attention to how information was coming to me, whether by feelings, words, pictures, or some other mode. Because the words I heard sounded like my own voice, it was hard at first to believe that the information was coming from somewhere outside of me. Once I started doing verifiable practicing, as you will be doing, I finally had proof that the voice I heard was indeed from the animal.

Only a few times have the words sounded like someone else's voice. This happened once when I contacted an Alaskan grizzly bear. I was working from a photograph taken by a naturalist who was studying the bears. The voice I heard was distinctly British, and the sentence structure was quite different from my way of speaking. I have no idea why I heard a bear with an English accent, but I will never forget the experience. Even though I seldom hear accents or different voice tones, the phrasing of the words that come to me is often unlike my own style of speech. As I write down what I am receiving, I sometimes find myself automatically capitalizing phrases or words, or underlining them and adding exclamation points. When this happens, I feel confident that the information is coming directly from the animal.

You don't have to be able to visualize in order to communicate intuitively. If you do not visualize well, try using the other modes. It really doesn't matter which mode you use; they all work well. I've found, though, that people in my classes who say they can't visualize usually end up doing so once they've practiced for a while.

Knowing is an aspect of seeing. When information comes to you in this way, you have the experience of "seeing it all" or knowing everything at once. Some people seem to operate best in this mode.

Receiving messages encoded as intuitive taste and smell impressions is the least likely mode for a beginner to work in, though a few people use it exclusively.

Until you start practicing, you won't know which modes you feel most comfortable with. After a while, you may find that you have confidence in all the modes and can switch from one to another. At that advanced level, you would simply ask for the information in the mode you prefer. For example, you might ask a dog to show you an image of where he was before he got taken to the animal shelter. Or you might ask a horse to send you the emotions she feels about her trainer.

For now, when you are starting out, stick with the emotions. Perceiving emotion intuitively is probably going to be the easiest thing for you to do. It's also the mode you can fall back on if you ever get stuck or blocked. Ultimately, your mode of receiving will be unique to you as an individual; there is no "right" way to do this.

Quieting Your Mind

In order to receive information intuitively, whether from universal knowledge or directly from an animal, you have to have a quiet mind — not an easy thing in today's world. Many students complain that they can't quiet their thoughts and internal dialogue long enough to receive intuitive information. That's why I developed the basic techniques for focusing and connecting that you will learn in this chapter. I made them as simple and direct as possible. If you follow them, I believe that you will be able to slow down enough to connect emotionally and mentally with an animal and hear what the animal has to say.

Some Initial Questions

Many people ask whether it is necessary to close their eyes to communicate intuitively. I work with my eyes open with my own animals, but I often close my eyes when I want to focus in on a client's animal. Some animal communicators work exclusively with their eyes open, focusing on the ground or on a blank wall to reduce interference from visual stimuli. There are no rules about this; do what feels most comfortable to you.

Another question that comes up is: Isn't it best to do this communication with the animal present, rather than at a distance? There is a notion that talking face-to-face with the animal is easier and will be more accurate. That is not always so in my experience. When you are present with them, animals want to interact with you. They may try to get you to play with, pat, or feed them, which can make it more difficult to connect intuitively. Much of my work is done at a distance from the animal, and my results are just as reliable either way. At the end of this chapter, I will give you some exercises that involve connecting with an animal using only a photograph. In later chapters, you will do exercises with your friends' animals, and you can choose to do them face-to-face if you wish. Then you can compare your results to see if one method works better for you than the other.

TECHNIQUES FOR FOCUSING AND CONNECTING

In this section, I will first describe each technique, then make recommendations for how to use the techniques. You can try out each technique as you read it. At the end of the chapter, you will have a chance to use these techniques in some exercises with animals.

Slow Down

Concentrating on your breathing is a simple technique to help you focus your mind and slow down. Here is how I do it:

1. Breathe in as deeply as is comfortable (imagine breathing down to the base of your spine).
2. Hold the breath for a moment.
3. Consciously slow down your exhale.

Try this a few times, striving with each breath to slow down and get more comfortable. You may wish to make this a regular meditation practice. Just doing it for a few minutes a day can help you train yourself to be calmer and more focused. I suggest doing it at the same time each day, perhaps in the morning, so that it becomes a habit. You might also add an affirmation. On the inhale, you might say mentally, "I am," and on the exhale say, "calm." Or substitute any affirmation you choose.

Get Grounded

Being grounded means feeling connected to the earth. To do this, I imagine that I have an invisible, stretchy animal tail that goes through the floor and the ground all the way to the center of the earth. I imagine that this tail stabilizes me while allowing me to move about freely.

Have a Positive Attitude

There are a lot of pitfalls involved with intuitive communication, and your own attitude may be the biggest one. You can be your own worst critic, which is no help to intuitive development. I have seen people inhibit themselves to the point where they cannot even try to communicate anymore. That's why I came up with the following technique; it helps you get out of your own way. Here is how it works:

1. First, figure out which of your beliefs is holding you back from communicating intuitively. There will probably be more than one. Here are some common choices: I will fail; it's not real; I will be making it up; I can't do it, only other people can; it's too hard; it's impossible; people will think I am crazy. This is the short list. I will never say I've heard them all, but I've heard many such inhibiting beliefs. Do any of those beliefs fit you? If not, take out your notebook and

write down the negative and limiting beliefs that are holding you back.

2. Now come up with a positive statement that counteracts those beliefs. You could include just one belief or a few. For example, let's take the following two beliefs: "I will be making it up" and "It's too hard." Here is a statement that reverses them: "Hearing intuitively is really easy, and I get amazingly accurate results."

3. In your notebook, write down your positive statement to counter one or more negative beliefs that you are aware of. You will use this statement when you do the exercises at the end of the chapter.

Having a positive intention sets you up for success. Hidden negative beliefs, on the other hand, set you up for failure. Any problem you are experiencing can be transformed into a positive intention. Your negative beliefs will probably change and shift as you work through this book. Be ready to change your positive statements to match whatever negative beliefs are bothering you the most in the moment.

This process of consciously reversing your negative belief systems can help in any area of your life. Articulating your positive statements by writing them down or saying them out loud gives them the force and power needed to overcome long-held negative beliefs.

Activate Your Intuition

To activate your intuition, simply imagine that your whole body is opening up to receive intuitive impressions. Tapping into your intuition connects you to the collective mind or universal pool of knowledge discussed in chapter 2, on page 22. I think of universal knowledge as if it were a library that has a reference book for every question I might possibly ask. To access this library, I imagine extending my consciousness up out of my head toward the collective mind, somewhere above me. I like to see this as a shaft of light extending upward. If you do not visualize easily, just imagine the feeling of being connected to all the knowledge in the universe and having that vast resource at your fingertips.

Connect with the Animal

Connecting with the animal is a crucial step. First, you will need to see the animal in person or get a picture or a description of the animal. Try to get a complete description, including common name (not registered name), age, sex, breed, color, and markings. Once you have an image or sense of what the animal looks like, close your eyes and see or feel the animal in front of you — as if it were right there with you — regardless of how far away the animal may be.

Next, focus on your heart and imagine it full of love. Now open your heart and send that feeling of love to the animal's heart. Once you've connected with the animal, you are ready to start communicating.

HOW TO USE THE FOCUSING
AND CONNECTING TECHNIQUES

These techniques are intended to put you in the right state of mind to be receptive to intuitive impressions. The techniques again are:

1. Slow down.
2. Get grounded.
3. Have a positive attitude.

4. Activate your intuition.
5. Connect with the animal.

Here is how I would recommend using these techniques. If you have any problems focusing and getting quiet, I suggest that you use the "slow down" and "get grounded" techniques as a daily practice to retrain your mind to be focused and calm. You can get results by doing this for just a few minutes a day. Try doing it at the same time every day so that you make it a habit.

You may want to consciously use the two techniques — "have a positive attitude" and "activate your intuition" — when you first begin practicing with animals. However, your body will memorize these techniques eventually. Then you will be able to become focused, calm, and ready to communicate by just taking a deep breath.

The last step, "connect with the animal," is one I recommend that you use consciously with every animal you talk with.

Finally, when you finish your communication, it is a nice gesture to say "thank you" to the animal.

I use these techniques as a meditation every morning before I begin my consulting work with the animals. Then, for every animal I work with, I do the "connecting" step. I also regularly take a deep breath to remind myself to be focused and calm. The deep breath acts as encoded information to my body, sending the unconscious message to slow down, get grounded, have a positive attitude, and activate my intuition.

Two Methods for Requesting Intuitive Information: Direct and Indirect

There are two distinct methods for requesting that information come to you intuitively:

1. Direct: intuitively sending a question directly to another person or animal, and then recording the impressions you receive
2. Indirect: connecting with universal knowledge, asking for information, and recording whatever impressions you receive

In the initial exercises in this book, you will be working with my animals and with me. If readers were to use the direct method of inquiry, my animals and I might not get much sleep. Therefore, for these first exercises, I will have you use the indirect method — asking universal knowledge. In later chapters, once you have some practice, you will begin to work with your friends' animals. At that point, you will be working one-on-one with an animal, and it will be appropriate to switch to the direct method for requesting intuitive information.

It is a good idea to learn both of these methods. When I do consultations, I alternate between the two approaches as needed. I usually ask information of the animals directly, but sometimes animals don't know the answers to my questions; they don't know why they feel sick, what they need, or why they are behaving badly. In those cases, I seek the answers by tapping into universal knowledge. When I look into the future, I also use the indirect method of tapping into universal knowledge.

Whether you ask for intuitive information directly or indirectly, it will still be conveyed to you in one of the five modes: intuitive hearing, feeling, seeing/knowing, smelling, or tasting. You may find that you receive different information from the indirect route than from the direct route, but any difference will be slight.

Let's take the example of asking a dog if he likes cats. Using the indirect method, you would go through the steps for focusing and connecting, feel the connection from the top of your head to universal knowledge, and then ask to have information come to you about whether the dog likes cats. You may then receive a visual image of the dog licking a cat or of the dog and a cat curled up sleeping together, which you would assume is an affirmative response. You might even hear the phrase, "He adores them." Were you to ask the dog directly, the methods would differ only at the end, where instead of asking for the information to come to you from universal knowledge, you would specifically address the question to the animal, silently speaking his name. When you ask directly, the same information might come as a direct statement from the dog, such as, "Yes, I love my cats!" You might even see an image of the dog and a cat sleeping together or the dog licking the cat. With either mode, you will still do the step of connecting from your heart and sending love.

RULES FOR RECEIVING INFORMATION INTUITIVELY

Until now, I've been saying "there are no rules, do what you want, take this and change it if you like." However, I've found that there are a few rules that always seem to apply. The following guidance will help you be more successful:

1. Let Go of Your Logical Mind

Logic squelches intuition. To receive intuitive information, you have to let go of any tendency to figure things out logically or try to be "right." Instead, as you work to receive information intuitively, pay attention to every thought, impression, feeling, memory, image, word, or sensory impression that comes to you. Record it immediately. This is the intuitive information you are seeking. Bypass your logical mind, your academic training, and your conditioned thinking. Your job is simply to record this stream of consciousness as you become aware of it. Sometimes intuitive information will appear even before you go through the steps for focusing and connecting. That's fine. Whenever an impression comes to you, record it and continue scanning for more information. It sounds easy, and yet this is the hardest part of receiving information intuitively. Eventually, after some trial and error, you will be able to go with what you get rather than trying to come up with the "right" answer. The truth is that, in intuitive communication, there is no way to figure out the right answer. The only option you have is to recognize and immediately record what comes in. Following that advice will guide you toward success.

Here is an example of how logic can hinder you. In a beginning class, one of my students asked a dog what he liked to eat. She got an answer but changed it. What she then told the dog's person was that the dog liked beef kibble. The dog's person asserted that the dog had never been given a single piece of beef kibble in his life. Understandably, the student was disheartened. As I spoke with her about the exercise, I managed to discover that what she had actually seen intuitively was a scene of the dog eating a raw beef bone. At this point, the dog's person interrupted and said, "Oh, why didn't you say that?! We give him raw beef bones all the time." The student explained that she had changed the beef bone to beef kibble because she didn't think people would feed raw bones to dogs.

In another class, all the students who talked with my cat Hazel were informed by her that she loved to have me scratch her stomach. Later, in discussion with the students, I found out that all of them had decided not to report that information because they felt that they must be wrong; surely no cat would like to have her stomach scratched.

2. Don't Censor Anything

Essentially, what these students did was to censor their data. In the kibble example, the information came in clearly and accurately, but the student changed it into something she thought would be more logical and, therefore, potentially more correct. I've done the same thing many times, trying to make what I get intuitively fit better with what I know about reality. It is hard to break this kind of mental habit, but over time it will diminish. The less you censor the information that comes in, and the more you record your impressions as they appear, the more likely you are to be correct.

3. Record Everything

I find that if I don't record intuitive information as it comes in, I am likely to forget it. It doesn't serve much purpose to communicate and have nothing to show for it, so I make sure to write everything down as it comes in. This means that sometimes I write with my eyes closed. I am trying to get good at this, but occasionally I can only read what I wrote after a few minutes of studying it from different angles. To get around this, you can tape record your information or type it into a computer. I tried typing and found that it interfered with my concentration, but some people prefer this method. Experiment to find out which method you like best. The main point is: record everything, exactly as you receive it. You should have the feeling that information is coming into your brain and immediately being recorded, as if you were a stenographer or translator.

In summary, here are the hard and fast rules for receiving intuitively:

1. Let go of your logical mind.
2. Don't censor anything.
3. Record everything.

The Secret to Increasing Your Accuracy

Usually, when a beginning student is good at recording information and has a high level of accuracy early on, it's because she had some prior training or encouragement in intuitive development. I can always tell who these students are right away because they are more confident of their abilities and they get more details and are more accurate when they talk with an animal. Sometimes they will record whole pages of information when everyone else in class just got a word or a phrase.

Recently I had a beginning student who, while not particularly confident of her intuitive ability, was writing up a storm. She got incredible details and was highly accurate, and her pen never left the page. I asked her about this, and she said she had taken a class in creative writing and learned how to do a technique called "automatic writing." That was her secret to success, and I am passing it along to you.

The concept of automatic writing as employed in creative writing exercises is to capture on paper the stream of thoughts running through your consciousness. You write without stopping to read or correct anything. When you do this, you do not even stop to think. Your pen should be moving continuously throughout the entire exercise. Automatic writing, when done as a daily exercise, has the effect of freeing your subconscious and unconscious mind so that you can write easily and more prolifically. It helps people who have writer's block. It is also an easy, effortless way to gain access to your intuition.

Now you will try out the techniques in this chapter by doing some simple beginning exercises in intuitive receiving.

EXERCISES: RECEIVING INFORMATION

Exercise 1: Automatic Writing

Choose a certain time to practice automatic writing every day. Do this exercise on loose-leaf paper rather than using your notebook, as you may generate lots of pages of scribble in the process. Pick a time limit for your writing; ten to fifteen minutes would be best. Set your alarm clock or timer for that time interval, and begin writing. Your pen should not leave the page. You can write about any topic you choose, or simply start off writing with two words, such as, "I will...", and then keep writing until the timer goes off. Do not edit, revise, correct spelling, try to make the writing readable, or otherwise stop to correct your text. Go with your stream of consciousness, and train yourself to open up this way. Try this now, before you go on to the next exercises, to get a sense of what it feels like to do automatic writing.

Personality, Likes, and Dislikes

Using intuition to get to know an animal's personality, its likes, and its dislikes is relatively easy. Once you get the hang of it, you can do it over and over with different animals for practice.

On the following pages are photographs of three animals. For each animal, you will be asked to discern the animal's personality and likes and dislikes. You will work only with the photograph and the animal's name and gender. I purposely do not give the animal's age so that you won't be tempted to make any assumptions on that basis. However, let's say you are reading this book ten years after it was first published and one of the animals pictured here has since died. You can still do the exercise because you can use intuition to view events in the past and the future as well as the present. Using your intuition, you can tap into the universal storehouse of all knowledge, be it past, present, or future.

Remember that for the beginning exercises in the next few chapters, you will use the indirect method for requesting intuitive information by tapping into universal knowledge. Later on, when you begin working with your friends' animals, you will use the direct method for requesting information by addressing the question directly to the animal. Also, remember to record any intuitive information you receive.

To begin, go through the preliminary steps for tuning in (summarized below). You might want to tape-record these steps and play them back for yourself, leaving an appropriate pause between each step. Be aware of your connection with universal knowledge. Now ask to have the information you seek come to you as intuitive impressions. Shift your awareness to what impressions — feelings, images, ideas, and other perceptions — you are receiving. Record this information immediately. Make sure that you capture every single thought, image, feeling, or other sensation you receive; don't censor anything. As in the automatic writing exercise, recognize and record the first thing that comes to mind. Then go on to the next thing and the next, until your thoughts are still. You should have a feeling that there is a list of things coming in and that you have to record it quickly to make sure you get it all. Please do not stop to consider whether it's correct; that will be your undoing. Just record every single bit of it.

When you're done, you can check the answer key at the back of the book to see if any of what you wrote down is true. If you aren't getting any impressions, make your best guess. You should try to record some answer — at least one word — for each question for each animal.

Do the exercises for all three animals before you check the answer key at the back of the book.

Review: Steps for Focusing and Connecting

1. Slow down: take a breath, hold it a moment, and slowly release it.
2. Get grounded: connect to the center of the earth.
3. Have a positive attitude: set yourself up for success with a positive statement.
4. Activate your intuition: open to your intuition and connect to universal knowledge.
5. Connect with the animal: send love from your heart to the animal's heart.
6. Follow your intuition: record whatever comes in, no matter what.

Exercise 2: Cat

This cat is named Hazel. Study the photograph. Feel your connection to universal knowledge and ask to be given information about Hazel's personality. Record anything

and everything that you perceive after asking the question. Then ask to know what she likes and what she doesn't like. Again, your job is to record everything and anything that occurs to you, even if you think it is stupid, weird, obvious, or made up; record it. Also, ask about Hazel's age, then record that information. If you didn't get any impressions, make your best guesses before going on to the next animal. Do all three animals exercises before you check your answers.

Exercise 3: Dog

Study the photograph of the dog. Her name is Brydie. If you wish, go back through the steps for focusing and connecting. Otherwise, just take a deep breath and send love from your heart to her heart. Feel your connection to universal knowledge and ask to be given information about Brydie's personality. Record your impressions. Then ask to know what she likes and what she does not like. Record everything and anything that occurs to you. Ask about her age and record what you get. Make your best guesses if nothing is coming in. Then do the final animal exercise before you check your answers.

Exercise 4: Horse

Study the photograph. This horse is named Dylan. If you wish, go back through the steps for focusing and connecting. Otherwise, take a deep breath and send love from your heart to his heart. Feel your connection to universal knowledge and ask to be given information about Dylan's personality. Record your impressions. Then ask to know what he likes and  what he doesn't like. Record your impressions. Ask about his age and record that. Make your best guesses if nothing is coming in. Open your eyes and come back into an alert state of mind. Now turn to the answer key at the back of the book to check your answers.

Discussion of Your Results

If you got 60 percent correct answers or more, you are doing very well, as do some of the people in my classes when they try these exercises. An accuracy rate of between 20 and 60 percent would be expected and acceptable for a beginning effort; you are just learning, so give yourself a break.

If you got fewer than 20 percent correct answers, it could just be beginner's bad luck, like falling off your bicycle a few times before you get the hang of it. I encourage you to keep trying the exercises in upcoming chapters. On the other hand, something might be amiss. It may be that you have a very active internal critic. If you know that this is a problem for you, see chapter 7 on how to deal with the inner critic. It could be that my instructions aren't adequate, that the exercise is simply too hard for your current intuitive skill level, or that you learn better when you can work directly with a teacher. In any event, you might be able to learn better if you take an animal communication class and work with a teacher in person. Sometimes people do poorly on one exercise and well on another. If you did not do well, my advice is that you keep reading and try the exercises in the next few chapters. If your accuracy does not improve, you may want to try working with a teacher in person to learn intuitive communication. I am sure that you will enjoy reading the book anyway, and you will probably be able to come back and do the exercises once you gain a bit more confidence and skill.

Chapter Seven

The Critic
Within

When you tell people that you are learning how to talk to animals, a fair number will be interested and curious; they may even ask for help with their animals. But a few will probably get nervous and try to pretend they didn't hear what you said. Others will narrow their eyes, scrunch their noses, and say, "Oh, how interesting," or simply, "Oh." Then there are those who will ask, "You mean like Dr. Doolittle?" instantly reducing you to a character from children's literature. This crowd is also likely to ask whether you can come over and teach the dog to get a job so that he can start earning his keep. A small faction will forever treat you as if you were mentally incompetent.

Negative reactions are understandable. Intuitive communication with animals is completely unconventional. Science says it's impossible. It challenges fundamental societal beliefs, namely that humans are the only truly intelligent beasts and that all other life forms are less important. When you challenge the status quo, you may at best be greeted with doubt or ridicule. In the Middle Ages, those who professed to communicate in this way were even burned at the stake as witches. There are still people who consider intuitive work with animals and other non-human beings to be evil, though I can't see how something that promotes compassion for other life forms could ever be viewed as evil.

When I began working professionally in this field, the low regard expressed by some people was a serious problem. I found myself needing to be open about my work in order to advertise my services, but secretly not wanting to tell anyone what I did. I felt unsafe and vulnerable to attack for doing something so unacceptable to society.

Undoubtedly, your road will be easier than it was for those of us who started in this field a decade or more ago, because today there is far more interest in and acceptance of intuitive communication. I hope that you will encounter only the mildest forms of challenge from others. However, challenge in some form is probably inevitable.

Add to society's challenge the insecurity that you probably feel about your own fledgling ability, and you get a double dose of doubt just when you need it least. It's hard not to doubt oneself when beginning to learn intuitive communication. We've all been trained by the academic system and by society to be good doubters, especially when it concerns something as unbelievable as intuitive communication. I've had very few students who sail through the classes with no self-doubt. Those few who did usually had someone in their childhood who encouraged them to use their intuition and imagination. They were also unconcerned about what other people might think of their interest in animal communication. Would that we could all be so secure! I certainly wasn't when I started out.

Not only was I worried about what others would think, but I was certain that I had no ability whatsoever. It surprised me when another student in the class I was taking asked for my help with a problem she was having with her cat. I couldn't understand why she wanted my help; to my mind, I was just making everything up. I agreed to try, and went to her house to confer with an elderly cat who was refusing to come out from the dirt basement of the house to take her hairball medicine. The cat had been under the house for about twenty-four hours when I went into the basement to talk with her. Following behind me, as if I were the Pied Piper, came all the other animals of the house, who apparently wanted to see what I could do to help their friend. We all sat on a couch and chatted with her. I asked her what it would take for her to drink her medicine, and I got the impression that she would drink it if it were put in some cream. I left, promising her she would have her cream. About an hour later, the student called to tell me that the cat came out and lapped up the medicine *au creme.*

The student must have seen what I could not: that I had some real ability even though I thought I was a dismal flop. Now that I have taught for so many years, I see this as a common pattern in beginning intuitive communication students. When they first start out, people are simply unable to accept the evidence of their ability and accuracy. Being able to talk with animals and really hear them respond is so unbelievable to us that it sets off an internal dissonance that takes time to resolve.

You will probably have to grapple a bit with your inner critic in the beginning. Try to be patient with yourself and be realistic about your progress. Learning this skill is a multi-layered process.

You can't be an expert instantly, any more than you learned to ride a bicycle instantly. Realize that mistakes teach you something; study them and learn from them.

Find a way to believe in yourself even if others around you express doubt. The fact is, the more you believe in yourself the less you will encounter doubt from others. Instead, people will be interested and curious about what you are doing. I came to see that the criticism I got from the outside world was to some extent a reflection of the criticism I held internally.

Learning intuitive communication is more than just learning another language. As with any language, you will learn a new set of symbols, skills, and techniques. But in learning intuitive communication you must also learn to trust yourself, believe in the information you receive, accept the idea that you can never do this perfectly, and learn to respect yourself even if others do not. These kinds of lessons have a spiritual quality. That's why I tell people that learning intuitive communication can become a journey of self-transformation.

YOUR INTERNAL POLICE OFFICER

In her book *Awakening Intuition*,[1] neuropsychiatrist and human medical intuitive Mona Lisa Shultz states that the frontal lobe of the brain, which is responsible for critical thinking and judgment, is where our internal critic resides. It functions like a police officer, warning us not to say something stupid or do something silly. It is always trying to protect us and keep us socially acceptable. It does not fully mature until after childhood, which explains why children can be so unselfconscious. In adults, however, this part of our brain constantly monitors and inhibits our words and actions.

The left hemisphere of the brain is associated with logic and rationality, while the right hemisphere and temporal lobes are associated with feelings, sensory impressions, intuition, creativity, and instinct. The strength of any one of these parts of the brain can vary from person to person. All play an important role in intuition, and all must interact in balance in order for you to get accurate, detailed information when using your intuition. Too much frontal-lobe control, and you will feel inhibited when attempting to use intuition. Too much left-hemisphere control, and you will find it difficult to get past being logical and trying to figure things out, rather than letting go and allowing intuitive insights to come to you. Usually, when people start out, their frontal lobes go on red alert: "What are you thinking of? This is crazy! You can't do this; no one can! People are going to think you are weird!" Taken to the extreme, this kind of interference can prevent people from even trying to pursue intuitive communication.

OTHER COMMON BLOCKS TO INTUITION

Another block you may encounter is the fact that in order to verify the information you get intuitively from an animal, you will have to divulge your answers. This process is treacherous for most of us who went through the public school system and remember how it felt to give the wrong answer or to flunk a test. Intuitive communication has the unpleasant feature of always requiring you to put yourself on the line; there is no other way to do this work. You have to tell people what you receive and let them verify its accuracy.

This impediment is compounded by the fact that you will never be right all the time. No matter how much you practice or how far you go with intuitive communication, you will always have the experience of being inaccurate some of the time.

Your own personal belief systems are another potential barrier to the intuitive process. Here are some negative beliefs that I have heard from my beginning students. You may recognize your own among them:

- I won't be able to do this.
- I can't get my mind to be quiet and still.
- I can't hear the animals talk to me in words.
- I don't visualize well.
- I am just making things up.

Your negative beliefs about the process or about your ability can hinder your progress. Identifying and then releasing personal beliefs that stand in your way is important, especially for the beginning student.

IDENTIFYING AND CLEARING YOUR BLOCKS

I have devised several tactics for clearing the blocks that may hold you back from communicating intuitively. Clearing your blocks is an ongoing part of intuitive communication; when you clear a block, a new one can come in. That is the nature of learning this skill and it can be a frustrating experience.

Before you can clear your blocks, you must first identify them by analyzing your feelings and motivations. If you search, you can usually find the core beliefs that cause you to feel a certain way or to act as you do. Here is an example of a session I did with a student to identify her blocks:

Janice Morikawa had taken a number of classes from me, and I thought she was doing pretty well with intuitive communication. But one day when we were doing a private session, she told me that she felt really tense in her stomach whenever she tried to communicate with the animals. Also, she had the feeling that it wasn't right to pry into the personal lives of the animals. We discussed this and discovered that when she was growing up, truth was off limits in her family. It was not acceptable to talk about how someone really felt. When Janice asked an animal a question like, "How do you feel about your person or your trainer?" she was transported back to a childhood in which asking about true feelings was unacceptable.

She also realized that, because of her experiences in school, she had a fear of being wrong. Finally, she felt that she wasn't getting enough details and verifiable "hits," although that was not my perception. Once she identified her blocks, we were able to come up with appropriate remedies from the following list.

The Remedies

One or more of the following techniques may help you deal with your personal blocks to intuitive communication.

Reverse Negative Beliefs

Many blocks stem from negative beliefs. If you feel that you aren't getting accurate answers, it may be because you think, for some reason, that you can't be accurate. One useful tool for moving blocks out of your way is to identify the inhibiting belief and turn it on its head. You can do that by making a positive statement that reverses the belief. For example, Janice needed to counter her beliefs that looking at the truth was not safe, that she was getting wrong answers, and that she was not getting good details. She came up with the following positive statement:

I help animals by talking to them, and I have fun getting really accurate, detailed information.

Janice can reverse her negative beliefs by saying this positive statement whenever she practices with the animals or whenever she catches herself mentally replaying those negative beliefs.

To sum it up, here is the formula for constructing a positive statement:

1. Identify the belief(s) you wish to change;
2. Come up with a statement that reverses the negative belief(s);
3. Phrase your positive statement in the present tense as if it were your current belief and experience;
4. Use this positive statement when you practice intuitive communication and any time you find yourself dwelling on the negative.

Make a Deal with Your Inner Critic

If you have an overactive internal police officer operating in your frontal lobe, you will feel that you are always censoring and stifling yourself — judging, criticizing, and generally not letting any intuitive information in the door. One way to short-circuit this situation is to make a deal with your inner critic. As an experiment, propose that instead of judging and censoring, your critic will just help you receive and capture information. You can set a time period of three months for this experiment. The rules are that your frontal lobe has to take a back seat and simply function as your assistant to help you capture every fleeting piece of intuitive information that comes your way. Then, at the end of the experiment, you can evaluate the results.

Use Positive Training Techniques on Yourself

In her book *Don't Shoot the Dog,* Karen Pryor explains the basics of positive training and clicker-training with dolphins and dogs. She recounts the story of a friend who decided to try clicker-training on himself to improve his tennis game. Instead of beating himself up for errors and bad strokes, he focused exclusively on what he was doing well. Whenever he fired off a good serve or executed a good stroke, he would pat himself and say, "Good job!" As he continued to focus only on how well he did, his game improved to the point where he was winning most of the time. I suggest that you try this on yourself. It is free, easy, and fun. You can use it for your intuitive communication practice or for anything else you are trying to master. The rule here is that you have to acknowledge every little success and completely ignore any failure. Make this a big deal. Give yourself a reward for doing any piece of an exercise well, getting any bit of it correct. Put a star next to your correct answers in your practice notebook and tell others how well you are doing. No one else can encourage you this way; you have to do it yourself.

Go with Your First Impressions

The best technique I can recommend for freeing your intuitive ability is to make a point of going with your first impressions. This means being fully alert for any slight impression that surfaces in your consciousness and capturing that impression rather than censoring and discarding it. You can even say to yourself, "What am I getting? What's coming in?" Then accept the first impression that comes to you.

Make Your Best Guess or Fall Back on Feeling

If you get stuck while you are practicing and you just aren't getting any impressions, there are two things you can try. First, try guessing. Make your best guess, and then check your answer. At least by guessing you are moving forward rather than staying stuck.

Second, try using your intuitive feeling mode and working from there to retrieve information. This mode is usually the easiest one for people, so if you are stuck it may help get things moving again. When searching for impressions using the feeling mode, everything will be based on how you feel and on what you feel the animal is feeling.

Take the Pressure Off

When you begin to practice intuitive communication by asking verifiable questions of a friend's animals, have your friend tell you the answers before you reveal what you got. Then you can share your answers with your friend if you so choose. Explain to people that you are just a beginner and that you might not be very accurate. Of course, this isn't true — I am amazed at how well people do when they are just starting out — but say it anyway to take the pressure off yourself.

Remember the clicker-training technique: Be very happy with whatever you get right, and ignore everything else.

Avoid Critical People

Being around people who aren't supportive can be a big problem. It is probably wise to avoid discussing what you are doing with people who are likely to be critical. After you develop some confidence in your abilities, you can let them know about your discoveries. If you happen to be living with a critical person, just don't discuss your practice with that person until you feel more confident.

Be Positive

If you are doing a daily breathing meditation, add a positive statement. For example, on the inhale you could say "I am" and on the exhale "very intuitive." Then, once you finish your meditation, imagine yourself doing intuitive communication for a friend's animal and getting good responses and results. See or feel this as if you were in a movie, and make it as real as you can. This technique can be used for anything you wish to create in your life.

EXERCISES: UNDOING BLOCKS

Exercise 1: Identify and Remedy Your Blocks

Being positive is one of the remedies listed above for removing a block. To try it out, start by identifying and recording some negative feelings or beliefs that you have about your ability to communicate intuitively. Pick two that you really want to change right now. Rephrase those beliefs so that you reverse them and make them positive, present-time statements. For example, "I am making this up" would turn into "I get really accurate, verified information." Another example would be "This is too hard for me," which would turn into "Intuitive communication is easy and fun for me." Now you can use these positive statements to bolster your confidence before you try an exercise or whenever you start to feel insecure.

Skim through the previous section on remedies again and pick one of the other techniques listed there that appeals to you. Try it out and keep a record of whether it helps you improve your skill.

Exercise 2: Practice on a Person

Sometimes people have an easier time doing the "personality, likes, and dislikes" exercise with a person instead of an animal. You already know what I do and some things about me, but you don't know what I like (including hobbies) and what I don't like. So try doing this exercise to intuitively pick up information about my likes and dislikes.

Start by looking at my picture on page 99. Then get focused. To do this, you can go through the steps for focusing (see chapter 6, pages 85–89) or you can just take a deep breath to focus yourself.

Remember that for the exercises you do with me or my animals you are asking for the information indirectly, from universal knowledge. Feel the connection to universal knowledge and ask for information about what I like and don't like. You can have your eyes open, looking at the photograph, or you can close your eyes to do this. Record every single impression you get. Continue on to the next exercise before you check your answers in the answer key at the back of the book.

Exercise 3: Try Again with an Animal

Try assessing personality, likes, and dislikes again, this time working only from a description of an animal. This time you will work with my neutered male dog, whose name is Bear. He looks a lot like Brydie (the black dog pictured in chapter 6 on page 98), but he is a little shorter and stouter and does not have a white spot on his face. Focus and then connect from your heart to his. Feel your connection to universal knowledge, and ask for impressions of Bear's personality. You can have your eyes open or closed to do this. Then ask to know what he likes and what he doesn't like. Record anything and everything that occurs to you. Ask about his age, and record what you get for that. Now come back to your normal waking state and check your answers in the back of the book.

Part Three

Advanced Techniques

Chapter Eight

Better
Reception

I continually search for and try out new methods to make intuitive communication easier and more accurate. I suggest that you do the same: Take any classes that you find intriguing and read every book on the subject that interests you; all of it will help you improve your abilities.

Now that you've tried out the basic steps and had a few experiences with communication, you can try exploring some of the more advanced techniques I will describe in this chapter. When I've been asked to do intuitive communication with animals in tense situations, these advanced techniques really helped.

In particular, I am thinking of a recent horse dressage and jumping show I attended. A distraught mother came to my booth and asked me to talk to her daughter's horse. It appeared that both horse and rider had started out the season doing well, but the horse was now refusing jumps and both horse and rider had experienced several falls. The daughter was in a panic about the prospect of falling on the course, and her mother was at a loss for what to do. I had about ten minutes to talk with the horse while the girl washed him between events.

I grabbed my clipboard and got focused en route to meeting the horse. When we got to the wash rack, I immediately connected with the horse and began speaking. He clearly told me that he could "jump the course with his eyes closed." He said that he was hesitating and refusing the jumps because he was not sure that the girl really wanted to go over them. He showed me that she was tensing up right before a jump and that she was leaning to the left, which was making him lose his balance.

I reported all this to the girl, telling her that I thought her best approach would be to completely relax, focus exclusively on her balance, tell her horse that she trusted him, and let him take care of her. When I related the part about leaning to the left, she gasped and said, "That's just what I do! How did you know?" I said, "Well, your horse told me."

She and her horse did very well at the show that weekend. They covered the entire cross-country course without any refusals. The girl later told me that at one point she slipped in the saddle and felt that she might fall, but her horse stayed perfectly balanced and slowed down slightly, allowing her to regain her seat. They didn't even get a penalty for that, and they won fourth place in their stadium-jumping competition. When I saw them afterward, she exclaimed, "He took care of me! He really took care of me!" As I patted him, I got a wonderful feeling of his complete satisfaction with what he had just accomplished.

SIGNATURES OF INTUITIVE INFORMATION

One way to increase your accuracy is by noting whether the information you receive has any of the three common signatures of intuitive information:

1. Immediate Information: The information comes in very quickly.
2. Unusual Information: The information is something you would not have made up in your wildest dreams.
3. Information of High Certainty: You have a strong feeling of certainty about the information.

If you recognize one of these sure signs, then you should make a special effort to record the information exactly as you received it. You can be fairly certain that it will turn out to be accurate. Following are some examples of these signature characteristics.

Immediate Information

Sometimes students remark that they get intuitive impressions about an animal even before I identify which animal we will talk with or what questions will be asked. That's how intuition works; it can be totally wild and unpredictable. I had that experience once when I was doing a home visit with an unruly parrot. As the woman explained the problems she was having with the parrot, an image of a gray kitten flashed into my mind. I promptly dismissed the image, thereby ignoring my own good advice about paying attention. When I spoke with the parrot and asked what was wrong, the bird again showed me this image and said she wanted a gray kitten. That had to be wrong, I thought. How could a parrot want a kitten? I searched for other causes for her behavior, but could only come up with the one issue: she really wanted a gray kitten. Expecting to be told that I was way off the mark, I gave my results to the woman — who then related that the parrot had recently lost her longtime companion, a gray female cat.

Unusual Information

When he was alive, I used my dog Dougal, an Irish Wolfhound mix, to teach my students about recording information no matter how strange it might seem. I had them ask Dougal what he did with water that made me laugh. A good 70 to 80 percent of the class would report one or more of his funny behaviors, such as (1) sticking his front foot in the water as he drank from the bowl, (2) putting his nose under water and blowing bubbles in his water bowl, and (3) chasing bugs around in shallow ponds and creeks with his nose under water. None of these behaviors is typical, logical, or predictable — although I have heard of some fish-chasing dogs. Most of the students felt that they had gotten something really silly that couldn't possibly be correct, but they wrote it down anyway because I was insisting that they record all results.

Information of High Certainty

When information falls into this category, you just know inside that it is right. You feel it so definitely that there is simply no doubt. This happens to me occasionally. In one instance, I was working with a cat who entered a stranger's car and was carried away. No one knew where he went. When I got in contact with him, he showed me that he had been let out of the car and I got the impression of an area about ten miles to the south of his home. The cat said that he was coming home and that he knew the way.

He was emphatic that he was coming home; I heard him say that over and over. I knew inside that he would find his way home, which he did within a few days.

IMPROVING RECEPTION

All of the techniques described in the next section can help you improve your intuitive reception skills. I collected them by reading, going to classes, working with people in the intuitive arts, and generally scrounging around. As you continue to practice, doing the exercises at the end of each chapter, try adding some of these techniques to see if they help you.

Become Aware of Your Intuitive Receptors

In his book *You Are Psychic,*[1] Pete Sanders, Jr., speculates that we have invisible intuitive or psychic sensory receptors similar to our physical sensory receptors. He describes receptors for feeling, hearing, seeing, and knowing intuitively. According to Sanders, the invisible intuitive receptor for feeling is in the region of the belly. I think there is another one located in the area of the heart. The intuitive hearing receptors, he says, are like invisible ears situated just above our real ears. The middle of the forehead is the site of the receptor for seeing images sent intuitively, and the crown of the head is the receptor for receiving information as knowing, in which you get the whole picture of an animal's life or situation all at once.

When you are communicating intuitively, assume that you actually have these receptors that, although invisible, are as functional as your eyes, ears, and other sensory organs. Imagine the feeling of opening each of these receptors to receive information intuitively.

Alpha, Beta, Delta, Theta

Researchers who measured the brain waves of people engaged in intuitive work observed that such people were functioning in the theta brain-wave state.[2] "Theta" is the state we're in just before falling asleep and as we wake up. Three other brain-wave states have also been recorded in the laboratory: "beta," the brain-wave pattern that corresponds to our normal waking state; "alpha," the brain-wave pattern that corresponds with a meditative state of mind; and "delta," the state we are in when dreaming. Think of how you feel right before you drift off to sleep or when you awaken. You can strive to achieve that state when you communicate intuitively.

One technique I've devised for doing this is to give the brain a somatic cue to go into a theta brain-wave state. When you fall asleep, your eyes roll upward. To some extent, you can elicit the theta brain-wave state by closing your eyes and gently rolling them upward a bit. Just do this once, and very gently. Don't force your eyes or try to hold this position. Essentially, you are giving a subtle somatic suggestion to your brain to go into a theta state. I like to combine this slight upward rolling of my eyes with visualizing a connection from the top of my head to universal knowledge.

In order to achieve a theta brain-wave state you must be relaxed. Try this technique to relax yourself, especially if relaxing is hard for you. Begin by breathing more deeply and slowing down your exhalation. Then, with each exhalation, consciously relax a part of your body, starting with your feet. Breathe in, then on the exhale feel all the tension in your feet — the joints and muscles — release and flow out of your feet. Now move to your ankles and lower legs and go through the same breathing and relaxing process. When you move up into your torso, imagine relaxing your internal organs as well as your muscles and bones. When you get to your heart, imagine relaxing and releasing any emotional tension you are holding there. When you get to your head, imagine relaxing all your thoughts and worries and releasing them out of your head. You should now be exceptionally relaxed. If you like this exercise, do it frequently. Along with giving you better access to your intuition, it will improve your overall well-being.

Resist Making Assumptions

I treat new animals I meet the same way I treat new people: I try not to make any assumptions based on appearances. I strive to have an open mind and to appreciate the unique personality of each individual. I don't succeed at this all the time. Of course, if I get any kind of negative intuitive impression, I don't ignore it. In any interaction with a person or an animal, if I were to begin to feel unsafe I would make the prudent assumption that for some reason that individual may be a threat, and I would act accordingly.

Whenever I slip and prejudge an animal based on species, breed, sex, or age, my assessments are usually incorrect. Dog rescue people know that not all golden retrievers are friendly, and horse people know that not all Arabian horses are high-strung. Try to recognize your prejudices, and resist acting on them.

Nothing's Coming In

The trick to catching information is to recognize that every single impression and sensation you perceive is potentially valid information, even if it seems off the subject, weird, nonsensical, obvious, or mundane. To be a good receiver, you need to constantly ask yourself, "What am I getting? What else am I getting?

What feelings do I have? What images, thoughts, memories, physical sensations, words, sounds, or smells am I getting?"

Pay attention and record every impression, sensation, memory, image, and perception that comes to you when you are communicating intuitively. If you can't get anything and feel blocked, record that. When you check later with the animal's person, you may learn that the animal is shut down and closed off to everyone, which is why you were feeling blocked during your communication. If you find yourself thinking about your bills, record that fact. It might turn out that the person has money worries and the animal is concerned about it. If your back itches, record that. If you are distracted by noises, record that. You never know what will turn out to be relevant.

If your mind goes off on a tangent or you think of some personal memory, record that. What you're thinking about may relate to the animal's current situation in life. You can even label your intuitive information as "something I am making up," but just be sure to record it anyway. Then check with the animal's person to see if any of your information is relevant.

Assess Your Style

Start to observe how you work when you communicate intuitively; evaluate your personal style. What is your best mode of reception? Are you more visual than auditory? Do you usually feel things or simply know the information? Begin to notice these characteristics in your style of receiving intuitively. In your notebook, make a record of your answers to the following questions:

- Which mode of reception is easiest for you — feeling, seeing, hearing, knowing, tasting, smelling?

- What most frequently interferes with or stops your process?
- What aspect of this work is most difficult for you?
- What do you get that confirms a connection with the animal?
- What cues do you get when you are accurate?

If you find yourself feeling stuck or frustrated, always revert to using the mode of reception that is easiest for you.

Work with a Guide

Some people are more oriented toward spiritual issues and pursuits. If this describes you, you will want to read this section. If not, then skip to the next topic.

Many people believe that each of us has unseen guides or helpers. These guides and helpers could be anyone: deceased relatives or animals, deities, spirit animals, or people. One student told me that her guide was a huge oak tree she knew and confided in as a child. In short, anything can be your guide; it's yours, after all. When you do intuitive work, you can call upon your guides to help you. I do this every day before I start my consultations. At this point, I have collected quite a few guides: animals, trees, people, even mountains. Each person's guides are unique; you may call on whoever seems appropriate. If you don't have a guide but want to find one, follow the exercise at the end of this chapter for finding your animal guide.

Speed Things Up

People either like structure or find it bothersome. If you feel that the steps for focusing and connecting are too slow, you can dispense with them in part or altogether. On the other hand, some people find that going through the steps is like a mental security blanket, helping them to calm down and connect intuitively. But if you are confident and want to speed things up, go ahead. Just start with a deep breath, connect with the animal by feeling the connection in your heart, and you're ready to go.

You don't even have to close your eyes. It might help, however, to focus on the ground or a blank area with your eyes open and learn to let your vision go into a soft focus. Your eyes do this naturally when you are daydreaming with your eyes open; in that state, you are no longer focusing on the scene before you and your eyes become relaxed.

STAYING CONNECTED

Here are some techniques for improving your connection with an animal during an intuitive communication session.

Imagine That You Are with the Animal

If you are having trouble connecting with an animal, try imagining that you are actually there with the animal. Again, you do not have to visualize to be able to do this; you can just feel as if the animal were present in front of you. Imagine calling the animal to you or approaching — if the animal is agreeable. Then imagine interacting: throwing a ball, giving a treat, or patting the animal. See what happens and what feelings you have about the animal. Make sure your heart is open, then connect with the animal by sending a feeling of love. You may find that you can discover a lot about an animal's personality through this process. Once you feel that you have established a relationship with the animal, begin your communication.

Ask for More Information

If you get information that is confusing or vague, you can always go back to the animal and ask for help. Ask the animal to send the information in a different way or to send more explanation. If you get only monosyllabic answers — as I did when I started out — just ask for more. Ask for complete sentences. Even when you do understand something, ask for further explanations. Sometimes people are so relieved to get some response, even if it is just "yes" or "no," that they don't think to ask for more detail. If you only get "yes" or "no" answers, go back to the animal and ask more questions. Why did the animal answer that way? How strong is that "yes" or "no" answer?

The automatic writing exercise described in chapter 6 is an excellent way to increase the flow and level of detail of your intuitive communications. If you are having problems getting information, I suggest that you practice automatic writing every day.

Address Resistance

Sometimes you will encounter an animal who is difficult to connect with. You may feel that you are getting nowhere, or the animal may actually tell you that he does not want to talk. In a consultation I did with a cat one time, I kept seeing an image of the cat turning its back to me and completely ignoring me. When I told the people attached to this cat what happened, they burst out laughing and explained that the cat did that to every visitor who came to the house. They said the cat thought she was too good for everyone but them.

There are many reasons why you might experience resistance on the part of the animal. The main one is fear. If people have previously mistreated an animal, you become just another possibly dangerous human even if you are connecting from a distance and present no actual physical threat. If you have this experience, back up and start over. Open your heart again so that the animal can sense that you are trustworthy. Explain your intentions to the animal, then ask why the animal does not wish to talk. Have a discussion about this with the animal and see if you can resolve the situation.

Sometimes the animal does not want anyone to know what he has to say. If that is the case, promise to keep the animal's information secret, keep your promise, and work to help the animal if you are able. If the animal is still resistant, say "thank you" and do not disturb him further. Send healing love and then disconnect emotionally.

Focus the Wandering Mind

If your mind starts to wander, or if you feel the connection weaken, go back to the step in which you interact physically with the animal in your imagination and reconnect on that level before going on. If your mind wanders a lot, it may help to practice the breathing meditation every day to train your mind to focus better. Doing yoga is another excellent way to learn to focus. If you find that you are always too sleepy to concentrate, you may have physical problems that need attention; chronic lack of sleep will also prevent you from being able to focus. If you simply have an ongoing tendency to nod off when you close your eyes, do your intuitive communication with your eyes open. Shift your gaze to the ground or a neutral backdrop and let your eyes relax into a soft focus. That will prevent you from slipping into sleep.

EXERCISES: DO YOU LIKE...?

The following exercises are the next level up from the beginning exercises you did in the previous chapters. I call these the "do-you-like exercises." In these exercises, you use your intuition to find out whether an animal likes or does not like a specific thing. For example, you might ask a dog whether he likes children or riding in cars.

I am going to start out by giving you a do-you-like exercise for me. Then I will give you one for Brydie, my dog, with whom you worked in chapter 6.

Before you begin each of the following "do-you-like" exercises, you can do the short or long version of focusing and connecting. You may also want to incorporate some of the advanced techniques you learned in this chapter. Here is the short version for focusing and connecting:

Take a deep breath, feel your connection to universal knowledge, feel your heart connect with the animal, and (with your eyes open or closed) begin communicating.

Here is the long version, which you might use if you are feeling unsure about your intuitive ability.

Summary: Steps for Focusing and Connecting

1. Slow down: take a breath, hold it a moment, and slowly release it.
2. Get grounded: connect to the center of the earth.
3. Have a positive attitude: set yourself up for success with a positive statement.

4. Activate your intuition: open to your intuition and connect to universal knowledge.

5. Connect with the animal: send love from your heart to the animal's heart.

6. Follow your intuition: record whatever comes in, no matter what.

Whichever version you use, remember to say "thank you" after you finish your conversation with an animal.

Exercise 1: Do You Like...? (Marta)

Tap into universal knowledge and ask to receive intuitive information about whether I like the things listed below. Go with your feelings about this. Imagine me in the situation described and see what comes to you. If you don't get anything, make your best guess; you have to write something down.

- Skydiving (jumping out of a plane with a parachute)
- Cooking
- Going to my high-school reunion
- Getting up early
- Swimming in the ocean
- Licorice

Now go on to Exercise 2 before you check the answer key in the back of the book.

Exercise 2: Do You Like...? (Brydie)

Tap into universal knowledge and ask for intuitive information about whether Brydie likes the things listed below. Go with your feelings about this. Record everything. If nothing comes to you, make your best guess.

- Going in the water: Imagine her in a shallow pond, a creek, at a lake, and at the ocean. How does she act in those places? Does she appear to like the water? Does she stay out of it? Does she appear to want to go swimming? Would she be chasing a ball or stick? What do you see or sense?
- Children: Imagine her with children of different ages and see how she reacts. What images or feelings come in?
- Carrots as treats: Do you see or sense that she likes or dislikes them?
- Being brushed and combed.

Check your answers to Exercises 1 and 2 in the answer key at the back of the book.

Exercise 3: Do You Like...? (Friends' Animals)

Now it's time to try practicing your skill by communicating with your friends' animals. Tell your friends that you are doing experiments in intuitive communication and ask if you might work with their animals. Make sure to let your friends know that you are just starting out and that you might not be highly accurate; that will take the pressure off you. Select at least two different animals to work with. Go to see the animals, or get a description and get each animal's name, age, and gender. Ask your friend to come up with a list of "do-you-like" questions for the animal — some things about the animal's preferences that your friend knows but you don't. If your friend can't think of any questions, pick do-you-like questions from the list provided in chapter 9. Make sure the questions have "like/don't like" answers.

The technique you use now will be the direct method for retrieving information. You will focus and connect (short or long version) as you did before. But now, after tapping into universal knowledge, go ahead and talk to the animal directly when you ask the questions. Now you can use the technique of imagining that you are seeing the animal in front of you on a big screen. Say the animal's name to yourself and imagine interacting with the animal. You might imagine patting the animal or giving a treat. When you talk, you will think the question to the animal. For example, you would mentally think something like this: "Sasha, tell me whether you like cats, and please make your answer really clear. Thank you."

After you've asked a question, wait to see what information comes in. If you don't get anything, mentally explain your difficulty to the animal and ask if he can make his answer clearer. You might also imagine the animal in a scenario, as you did with Brydie. Then watch what happens as if you are viewing a movie. If you still don't get anything, go with whatever your gut feeling tells you, and make your best guess. You have to record something. When you are all finished, thank the animal and come back out of the intuitive mode into your normal waking state.

Now check back with your friend. Instead of telling your friend the answers you received, you could ask your friend to tell you the answers. Again, this takes the pressure off you. Acknowledge and give yourself credit for everything you get right. Mark your correct answers. Ask about anything you got that your friend did not cover. You can do the "do-you-like" exercises with as many animals as you please.

EXERCISES: VISUALIZATION

Exercise 4: Finding Your Animal Guide

This exercise is designed to help you find and work with an animal spirit guide. Do the exercise if this is something you are interested in. You can do it in any one of several ways:

- Read through the exercise, then sit or lie comfortably with your eyes closed and take yourself through it from memory.
- Have someone read it to you as you sit or lie comfortably.
- Tape it for yourself and then sit or lie comfortably with your eyes closed and follow along with the tape you made. If you want to get fancy, you can add a slow drum beat in the background (if you have a drum, you can play the beat yourself; otherwise, you can play a tape of slow, soft drumming in the background to go along with the visualization). Make sure you allow for the pauses indicated in the text in parentheses.

Close your eyes. Take a deep breath. Imagine that you are walking along a path beside a creek. Feel the sun shining down, and smell the herbs and flowers along the creek. As you go along, you find that the path veers off through some trees. Keep following the path through the forest. As you follow the path, you notice that the trees start to thin out. There are fewer and fewer trees until the path opens out into a vast meadow. There are mountains in the distance. The day is so warm and the meadow so inviting that you decide to stretch out and take a nap. (Pause for twenty seconds but continue drumming through the pauses.)

You don't know how long you have been asleep, but something starts to awaken you. You become aware that you are no longer alone in the meadow. You realize that there is an animal there with you, but it feels totally safe and right. You open your eyes to see who it is. It may be an animal you have known in the past or an animal you have never met. This is your animal guide who has come to help you with your communication and in your life. Ask for this animal's name if you don't already know it. Ask why this animal came to help you. (Pause for thirty seconds.)

The animal will now take you on a journey to teach you what it is like to be that animal. To go on this journey, you need to change from your human form into the form of this animal. Begin to feel that happening. See your face changing and your nose, eyes, and mouth becoming like the animal's. Feel your feet and hands changing into those of the animal. Feel your skin and body change to be like the animal's. You may grow a tail if the animal has one. Feel yourself completely change into the form of your animal guide. Now follow your animal guide as it leads you on a journey to understand its way of life. (Pause for five to eight minutes.)

Tell your guide that it is time to start your return to the meadow. Come back into the meadow and begin to feel yourself shifting back into your human form. Feel your feet and hands returning to normal. Feel your body shift and your skin and hair turn back into your own. See your face shift as all of you returns to human form. Thank your guide for taking you on that journey. Ask if your guide has any advice for you before you leave. (Pause for thirty seconds.) Ask how and when you will meet your guide again. (Pause for fifteen seconds.) Ask how the two of you will work together. (Pause for fifteen seconds.) Now give your guide a gift of thanks. It could be a real gift, or a pledge or promise, or just your love. (Pause for ten seconds.)

Now begin walking back toward the path through the woods. When you turn to look back at the meadow, your guide is gone. Continue along the path until you get to the creek, then walk along the creek path until you get back to your body and the room. Stretch, open your eyes, and come back into a fully alert waking state.

Chapter Nine

Practice, Practice

So far, I've had you work with other peoples' animals to learn to receive information intuitively. It's harder to talk with your own animals because you know so much about them that whatever you receive seems like something you made up. So, in preparation for working with your own animals in the next chapter, I recommend that you practice a little more with animals you don't know well.

WAYS TO PRACTICE

You can continue practicing the two exercises we have done so far:

1. Determine an animal's personality, likes, and dislikes. Then check your answers.

2. Ask "do-you-like" questions. Then check your answers.

Those exercises are straightforward, and they will net you data that you can verify. There are many other ways to practice. You might imagine yourself as a reporter, approaching the animal as you would approach a person you were interviewing, and asking more open-ended questions. I have included some of these types of interview questions for you to experiment with at the end of this chapter.

If you are starting to feel confident, you might offer to do some problem-solving for your friends. Talk with any of their animals who are exhibiting bad or unexplained behaviors and learn what the animals have to say about themselves. Or work with an animal who seems to have emotional problems and see what you discover. You will find exercises for this type of practice at the end of this chapter, too.

It's up to you whether or not you practice; this course is completely self-directed. It is also up to you to choose the manner in which you practice. If you want to go off on your own and try something completely different from what I am suggesting, by all means do so — and let me know how it works for you.

PRACTICING OUT IN THE WORLD

You can practice with the animals you see as you go about your day — for instance, dogs around town, animals you meet while on a walk, or horses at your barn. When you are out and about, you probably won't have the opportunity to close your eyes, get really focused, or have your notebook handy. That's OK; you can still practice. All you need to do is mentally greet the animal and send a feeling of love. Then either look right at the animal or shift your gaze to the floor or some other neutral subject so that you won't get visually distracted. Now you are ready to ask a question or send a mental message to the animal.

One message you could send is a comment on something that you admire about the animal — looks, attitude, intelligence, or good health. Animals like compliments as much as we do. You might also tell the animal, mentally, that you are learning how to talk with animals — then see if anything happens. I have done this and have had an animal turn around and stare at me in complete disbelief. If you have the time — maybe while waiting in the vet's office — you might strike up a conversation. With your eyes open, go through the same introductions and then ask the animal why it came to the vet that day. Then you can ask the animal's person the same question to find out if your intuitive information is correct. I have done this kind of practice at the dog park while taking a break on the bench: I ask a dog I don't know to tell me her favorite foods. Then I ask her person what the dog's favorite foods are.

You could also ask the animal if she has a question for you or whether she has something she wants to tell you. Remember that you must assume that whatever comes back to you intuitively is from the animal. Otherwise, you will second-guess yourself to death. If you get a question or a statement, respond as best you can.

One final idea you might explore is working with another person or even a group of people. Perhaps you could work with a friend who is reading this book at the same time you are. Do the exercises together with the same animals and compare your results. Working with one or more people has the effect of enhancing intuitive ability.

The more you practice, the better you will get; it's that simple. Suzanne Martin has been practicing intuitive communication with animals for several years now and has gotten quite good at it. Here is a story she sent me about a recent experience:

I had an exciting weekend recently when I went with my horse to Ft. Worth to visit some friends. Late in the afternoon, we decided to go for a trail ride. As we headed out we heard an animal screaming and making a lot of noise. From past experience at my farm, I recognized it as the noise goats make when they're in trouble or separated from the herd. We kept hearing the cries on and off, but could not find the animal.

We rode for about forty minutes, and on our return we heard the cries again, even louder and more frantic. I yelled out, "Are you stuck?" I swear I heard a "yes" in the responding cry. Then I yelled, "Do you need help?" and again I heard the word "yes." Finally I called out, "Where are you?" In response I heard "here," and found myself drawn to look over my left shoulder. As I scanned the horizon, I was able to see what looked like an animal's head, way at the top of a hill at the intersection of two fences. Without thinking about it, I said to my friends, "There is a goat caught in the fence who needs our help to get out."

We rode over, and sure enough the goat had gotten his head caught in the wire fence, but there was no way for him to get out on his own. After we helped him out of the fence, he started walking in my direction making more noises, which I heard as "Thank you." I told him he was welcome and that he needed to go and find his herd so that he would not risk being caught by coyotes. With that he turned away, headed off, and started calling for his herd. This is one of the most amazing things I have ever experienced. I still recall how clearly I could hear the goat's messages. My friends know I am intuitive, but even they were blown away.

EXERCISES: TALKING WITH YOUR FRIENDS' ANIMALS

When you do these exercises, try to work with animals about whom you know nothing, or very little. Since all you need is a photograph or a description, you can work with friends of friends' animals or with animals from out of your area. If you work from a description, make sure to get the name (barn name for horses), age, breed, marking, and gender. You will use the description to form an image or to get a sense of what the animal looks like.

Before each exercise, go through the steps for the short or long version of focusing and connecting, which are summarized in chapter 8 (pages 129–130). Also, when you finish remember to thank the animal.

Exercise 1: Personality, Likes, and Dislikes

Directly ask the animal to describe her personality and tell you what she likes and dislikes. Record all your impressions. Check your answers.

Exercise 2: "Do-You-Likes"

Ask your friends to give you some specific, verifiable "do-you-like" questions for their animals. Directly ask the animal these questions. Record all your impressions. Check your answers.

EXERCISES: ANIMAL INTERVIEWS

When you interview an animal in one of the exercises below, you will focus on more open-ended questions that go beyond the "yes" or "no" answer format of the do-you-like questions you have been working with.

Exercise 3: Roving Reporter

Pick some open-ended questions from the question list at the end of this chapter to ask one of your friends' animals. Pretend that you are a reporter and interview the animal. Follow tangents if they come up. Record all your impressions. Check your answers.

Exercise 4: Tell Me About Yourself

Ask your friends' animals the following questions and record your impressions. Check your answers.

- What is special about you?
- What is your favorite activity?
- What do you do best?
- Do you like to be patted? If so, where?
- What makes you sad? What makes you happy?

Exercise 5: Tell Me About Your Person

Ask your friends' animals the following questions and record your impressions. Check your answers.

- Tell me what your person is like.
- What does your person do that makes you laugh?
- Is anything bothering your person right now?

- What would you change about your person if you could?
- What is your favorite activity with your person?

Exercise 6: Tell Me About Your Life

Ask your friends' animals the following questions and record your impressions. Check your answers.

- Can you show me or tell me what your home looks like?
- What animals, if any, do you live with?
- Would you want any more animals around? If so, what kinds?
- Is there anything in your life that has changed recently?
- What would you change about your life if you could?

EXERCISES: PROBLEM SOLVING

Exercise 7: Bad Behavior

Offer to talk with an animal who has a behavior problem. Find out from the animal what is wrong and why she is acting the way she does. Help the person find some positive methods for resolving the problem.

Exercise 8: Emotional Upset

Offer to work with an animal who is upset. Talk with the animal and find out why she is feeling poorly. Ask what she needs in order to feel better. Work with her people to find positive ways to help the animal.

Exercises: Out and About

It's best not do these exercises while driving!

Exercise 9: Pay a Compliment

With your eyes open, send the animal a greeting and compliment her about her appearance or anything about the animal that strikes you as noteworthy. Explain to her that you are learning to communicate with animals.

Exercise 10: Ask for Information

With your eyes open, ask the animal if she has a question she wants to ask or something she wants to tell you. Respond as best you can. Ask her specific questions — for example, why she's at the vet that day or what her favorite foods are. Then check your answers with the animal's person.

Exercise 11: Work with Another Person

Try doing some exercises with a friend or a group of friends, working with the same animals. Compare your answers and build your confidence.

Questions to Ask Animals

All Animals

- What do you like? What do you dislike?
- Is there anything you need or want?
- Do you like other animals of your species?

- Who are your best friends?
- Which people do you especially like?
- Is there anything you want to tell your person or me?
- Do you like children?
- Do you like any other kinds of animals?
- What is your favorite activity?
- What are your favorite places?
- What are your favorite toys?
- Do you like to go to the vet?
- How old are you?
- Do you have a favorite place to sleep?
- Describe your home — the place where you live.
- What are your favorite foods?
- Do you like playing in or going into the water?
- How are your manners?
- Do you like your name?
- Describe your personality.
- What is scary to you?

Questions for Dogs

- Do you like to chase cats?
- Have you gone to obedience class?
- Do you like to ride in the car?
- Do you go on vacations?
- Are you friendly to other dogs?
- Where do you like to go for a walk?
- Have you been to the ocean?
- Have you been to a lake?

Questions for Cats

- Do you hunt?
- Do you like your home?
- Are you an indoor or an outdoor cat?
- How do you feel about dogs?
- Do you have a cat box?
- What does your meow sound like?
- Do you talk a lot?
- Do you like music?

Questions for Horses

- Do you have a blanket for cold nights?
- Have you ever been mistreated?
- Do you mind going into a trailer?
- What do you eat?
- Do you jump?
- Have you had a baby? (for mares)
- Do you go on trails?
- Do you have a stall?
- Do you like your shoer?

Part Four

Practical
Applications

Chapter Ten

Talking with
Your Own Animals

If you live with animals, you've probably had this experience: your animal is staring at you, and you know he's trying to tell you something, but you can't figure out what it is. After I learned intuitive communication, I had that animal-staring experience with my two female cats, Jenny and Hazel. I had just taken a shower and was on my way to the bedroom to get dressed when I spied the two little girl kitties, sitting side-by-side outside the bathroom door just staring at me. I knew they had something to say, so I asked, "OK, you guys. What is it?" In response, I got an outpouring of sympathy: They felt so bad for me, they said, because I did not have fur and was not beautiful and sleek like they were. At least that's what I think they said! You see, that's the essential problem in talking intuitively with your own animals: It's hard to verify what you receive. This chapter will help you learn to trust what your animals are saying to you intuitively.

WHY IT'S HARDER TO TALK
WITH YOUR OWN ANIMALS

When you work with your own animals, you already know all about them — or at least you think you do. So when you try to talk with them, your logical mind can really interfere. You struggle with the feeling that you are making things up based on what you already know about your animals. Sometimes you can resolve this dilemma by getting confirmation from the animal: He will act differently after you talk, doing something physical to send a clear message that you have been heard. My sister Anne told me about her experience of this with her Shire-cross draft horse, Oliver. While he was engaged in his favorite occupation, eating, she said, "Oliver, if you are my true friend and we are as close as I think, please come over and give me kiss." She said that Oliver actually stopped eating — a miracle — then came over and nudged and cuddled with her. You can't always count on that kind of confirmation, but when you get it, it's absolutely convincing.

When you are practicing intuitive communication with an animal you don't know, it is usually easy to get verification; you just ask the animal's person whether you are right. When it's your own animal, though, there is no one to ask. I will give you some techniques for getting around this obstacle. However, the fact that you are emotionally involved with your animal can make it hard to be objective when communicating. If you are dealing with an annoying behavior or if your animal is in some kind of crisis, being dispassionate may not be possible. In such cases, I recommend getting assistance from a professional animal communicator.

HOW TO WORK WITH YOUR OWN ANIMALS

Start out by explaining to your animals that you are learning to receive intuitively and that you need all the help they can give you. Remember to talk with your animals as if they understand everything you say, just as a person would. Many of you are probably already adept at reading your animals' body language. You may even have thoughts pop into your head that you feel sure have come from your animals. Now the goal is to be able to hear them talk to you whenever you wish. Eventually, you should be able to have a conversation with your animal equivalent to the kind you would have with a person.

Here are two ground rules that will help you be a clear and concise receiver when working with your own animals:

Rule 1: If you think they are trying to talk to you, they are. If you get even the slightest notion, impression, or feeling that your animal has something to say to you, assume you're right. Take the time to stop and talk.

Rule 2: Whatever you get, assume it's from your animal. When you talk with your animal and ask for information, assume that whatever you receive in impressions, feelings, words, visual images, or sensations is information that was actually sent to you intuitively by your animal. Do not question or doubt the information; simply respond to it as best you can, as if it were absolutely real and accurate. If you don't quickly accept what you get, you will begin to second-guess yourself and end up in a mental knot.

Techniques

Here are some techniques for working with your own animals. I made up some of them, and my students suggested some to me. Try them and see what you like. Practice with your animals on a regular basis. Soon, hearing your animals' intuitive messages will feel like second nature.

Making Contact

When working with your own animal, you don't have to go through the steps for focusing and connecting; you are already connected. You can just start talking without any formalities. You can communicate with your eyes open, shifting your gaze to something neutral and going into a soft focus, or you can close your eyes if you prefer.

When you talk to your animal, remember that you can talk out loud or send information mentally as thoughts, feelings, or pictures. Your animal will receive the message no matter what mode you use and regardless of whether you are near or far away.

Ask for a Question or Opinion

In the beginning, when working with your own animals, it is best to keep things light and easy. Don't try to resolve your cat's scratching or your dog's barking problem as your first communication project. Instead, find ways to practice with your animals that will be enjoyable for both of you. One technique is to ask for a question. Asking if your animal has a question for you takes the pressure off. If no question comes in, ask again another day. If you do get a question, you must assume that it came from your animal and answer it as best you can. Then ask if there are any more questions. I like to answer my animals' questions out loud. Somehow, for me, that makes the whole process feel even more real. When you do this exercise, you may find yourself involved in a conversation with your animal without even trying.

You can also ask your animal to send you impressions. For example, you can ask to receive a feeling, image, or thought from your animal. Sometimes this exercise can naturally shift into a back-and-forth intuitive exchange. My favorite technique is to ask the animal's opinion or advice about something. This could be anything from opinions or advice about decorating to what you're doing with your life or what is happening in the world. Just remember to assume that whatever advice or opinion you receive really came from your animal. Always respond as best you can.

Believe What You Receive

The real trick to having two-way conversations with your own animals is to believe what you receive. The following stories demonstrate how this technique has worked for others. Sarah Reid sent me this story after she took my beginning class. Sarah now communicates intuitively every day with her twenty-year-old Arab gelding, Verdi. She shares this story:

> Verdi and I were really tired after a four-mile ride at Point Reyes, so I got off and walked him the last mile to the parking lot and decided to try asking him how he felt. He told me that he was tired but felt good, and that his feet were really tired and a little sore. I asked him to show me his favorite part of the ride, and he showed me an image of when we were flying through the forest at a really fast trot. Then I asked him to drink really well for me when we got back, and I told him how much I appreciated him. It felt great to be able to check in with him like that. Now

I know I can do that during endurance rides, which will be really helpful.

I did have doubts about one conversation Verdi and I had, though. Verdi went lame in front recently, and I asked him which foot hurt. He told me that it was his right front foot, and I got an impression of a stone bruise. Then I had a vet come out, who said that Verdi probably had an abscess forming in his left front foot. I thought that perhaps I didn't hear Verdi correctly. We pulled the shoe, but he never got an abscess. After two weeks, we put the shoe back on and he was sound. Then, with his next regular shoeing, the farrier said that the right front foot showed white line disease, which was probably the result of an irritation like a stone bruise on that foot. So I should not have doubted myself!

Verdi talks to me more now, too, both verbally and by touching me with his nose. Some days he's almost in the way with his nose! If I fail to talk with him, he pushes me to get my attention. It's like he's saying, "So Sarah, what's going on with you today? Talk to me!" Before, I thought that Verdi was "only an animal." Now I know how emotional he is in general, and about me in particular, and I can read his emotions. I know what makes him happy, and that is all I want for him.

Verdi comforts me often when I tell him I am feeling bad. One Saturday when I went to ride him, I was very sad because our dog had died the night before. I cried on Verdi's shoulder and he "hugged" me with his head and comforted me. I told him that I needed him to take care of me that day and to take me for a nice little ride in the park to make me feel better. He was an angel. He was very gentle and also made me laugh. That was one of our most special rides together.

Myrna Krohn, whose story follows, developed an ability to hear her horses on her own after she and I worked together on some consultations. You may remember Myrna and her horse, Bear, from chapter 5. Myrna now checks in intuitively with Bear when she is riding:

It's been a long time since we talked, and I thought you would like to have an update on Bear. He is a different horse! He is happy and relaxed in his work. The trainer comes here, and that makes all the difference with Bear. We still do the trail rides two days a week, and we practice dressage for three days with two days off to just do horse things. I take him on trail rides to visit the goats, longhorns, and donkeys; he's like a kid out of school. He's doing fourth-level dressage work and has turned into quite a dressage horse. We will begin showing fourth level in the spring. I promised him that I would not ask him to show unless he feels ready and confident.

I can hear Bear talking to me now when we school. One day he was having trouble doing a turn on the haunches to the right. He was also having the same trouble with the sweeps to the right in the trot and with the volte right in the canter. He kept trying to throw me to the right of his back. Then I heard him say, "Move your right shoulder back." I did as he requested, and everything fell into place. You could tell he was pleased with himself because he did his "happy dance" and wagged his head from side to side snorting to the world that he had fixed his rider.

Now, before either of us gets tense, we have a talk to see

what the problem is. He always puts in his two cents, but he will listen to me and, more times than not, will do as I suggest. I think the important thing is that he has a voice in what happens to him. I can feel it when Bear is trying to figure something out, and when he gets it he still has to do his "happy dance," which I used to think was disobedience.

Ask Inconsequential Questions

Another good technique when you begin talking with your own animals is to ask inconsequential questions such as, "What is your favorite color? What kind of weather do you like best?" Or use any such question that is neutral and has no significance for you. The point is to find questions that are fun. After you ask the question, assume that whatever impression you receive is coming from your animal.

Virginia Simpson-Magruder tried this with her paint horse, Magic, right after she had a private tutoring session with me. Before heading home from the class, she silently asked Magic from a distance what color he liked. She was surprised when she got the color blue as a response, because she really disliked that color. It made her think that the information probably really was from Magic. On the way home, she stopped in to buy Magic a new halter and saw a beautiful steel-blue halter that she even liked herself. When she put it on Magic, he seemed exceptionally pleased with her purchase and the color suited him perfectly.

Be Alert to Your Animals' Messages

Animals give us intuitive messages all the time; we just don't often hear them. We may respond to their messages anyway, perhaps by filling their water bowl or by opening the door to let them in or out, but we will assume that the action was our idea. To sensitize yourself to your animals' messages, become alert to your intuitive feelings and impressions about your animals. Turn up your internal awareness of your animals. Whenever you get a sense that they are trying to tell you something, follow that feeling and recognize its origin.

Myrna Krohn sent me another story about a different horse, Ecstaz, a warmblood gelding she recently bought. Ecstaz had been through a lot of stress and uncertainty in his life before he came to live with her. She writes:

> I was away from home with my sister for the birth of her son. When I returned, I went to the barn to say hello to everybody. But before I even walked through the door I had an awful feeling of dread; I knew something was wrong with Ecstaz. I went to him immediately and he put his head against my chest, like he always does, and closed his eyes. I held him and closed my eyes, too, and then I heard him. In the most pitiful, sorrowful voice he said, "Why didn't you tell me you were leaving me? I didn't know if you would be back."
>
> I stayed with him all day to reassure him that he was safe and that this will be his home for the rest of his life. I told him that if I leave for a short time, I will always come back. I think it is important for people to realize that if they are going to be gone for a period of time, they should take a few moments to tell their animals where they are going and when they will be back.

Just Sit and See What Comes In

Many of us are overachievers; we've been rewarded for overworking, being stressed out, and pushing ourselves to the limit. But those traits won't serve you well in the intuitive arts. You will have much better success if you dawdle, daydream, and just sit and do nothing. Take the time to just hang out with your animal with no agenda, no timetable, no program, and no expectations.

EXERCISES: TALKING WITH YOUR OWN ANIMALS

The following exercises incorporate all the techniques described in this chapter. Try them out and see how they work for you. If you have more than one animal, you can do these exercises with each animal. You can also do some of these exercises daily as an ongoing practice with your animals.

With your own animals, you should be able to just start talking without going through the focusing and connecting steps. But if you want to do those steps, they are summarized in chapter 8 (pages 129–130). Try experimenting with keeping your eyes open when you talk with your animals. Shift your gaze to the floor and go into a soft eye focus while you are listening intuitively. Use your notebook when you practice, and record your results.

Exercise 1: Explain What You Are Doing

Tell your animal that you want to have two-way intuitive conversations and that you are going to try several exercises to help yourself learn this skill. Ask your animal to help you as much as possible whenever you practice.

Exercise 2: Ask for Impressions

Ask your animal to send you the following items:

- A picture
- An emotion

- A word
- A physical feeling
- A smell
- A taste
- A thought

Exercise 3: Ask for a Question

Ask your animal if he or she has a question for you. Pay attention. Whatever question comes in, answer it as if it came from your animal. Then ask for another question until you've answered them all.

Exercise 4: Ask Inconsequential Questions

Ask your animal the following questions, or make up some of your own:

- What is your favorite color?
- Which of my friends/relatives do you like best?
- What do you dream about?
- Where would you like to go on vacation?
- What part of the year do you like best?
- If you could be any kind of animal, what would you be?

Exercise 5: Ask for Advice or Opinions

Ask your animal to give you some advice or to offer an opinion about something you are doing or something in your life — or about any other topic. Repeat out loud to your animal what you think you received.

Exercise 6: Improve Communication

Imagine your dream of how it could be when talking with your animal. Create a movie of this experience in your imagination. Make it as real as possible. Tell your animal that this is your dream and ask what needs to happen so that you two can talk this way. Now ask the following questions:

- Is there anything from the past you want me to know about?
- Do you have any problems that I should know about?
- How do you feel about me?

Exercise 7: Talk When They Want To

Heighten your intuitive senses when you are around your animals. See if you can sense how they are feeling as you go through the day. Be alert to subtle changes. If you get any inkling that they want to talk with you, take some time out to sit with them and ask what they want to talk about. Remember, when you work with your own animals you have to accept whatever comes in as accurate.

Exercise 8: Just Sit and See What Comes

Find a time when you have no obligations, no appointments, and no worries. Plan to spend at least half an hour just sitting with your animal. Observe your animal and let go of all expectations. Simply enjoy being totally present with your animal.

Chapter Eleven

Past, Present,
and Future

As you have now seen, there are many practical applications for intuitive communication. I use it frequently to help clients learn about the previous experiences of shelter animals and rescued animals whose pasts are unknown. You can also use it to help resolve animal behavior problems. Now that you've had some practice with hearing your animals talk intuitively, you can interview them to find out how they feel about things such as their names or the activities you do together. You can even experiment, using your intuition, to predict the outcome of future events related to your animals' lives. The exercises at the end of this chapter will give you practice in each of these areas.

FINDING OUT ABOUT THE PAST

Using intuitive communication to find out about a rescued animal's history can help both the animal and the adopting person. If an animal has been abused, it's important to find out what happened and to know what might trigger fears or memories of the abuse. These triggers can then be avoided or defused for the animal. You can also counsel and reassure the animal and find out what she needs in order to be able to trust and feel safe.

This approach proved useful for Jody and Mike Jones, who manage Homeward Bound Golden Retriever Rescue and Sanctuary, Inc., a nonprofit rescue organization in Sacramento, California. Jody called me about a male golden retriever named Dodger, who was too dangerous to place in a home. She and Mike were afraid to open Dodger's crate, and they even worried that he might bite through it. Dodger would not make eye contact with them, and when approached he became extremely vicious. I was called in to determine whether there was any hope of rehabilitating this dog. Jody and Mike were seriously thinking of putting him down — the first time they'd ever considered such a course of action.

When I talked with Dodger, I received images and feelings from his earlier life. I saw a small, fenced dog run and a woman who was terrified of him; the woman poked him with a stick to fend him off while throwing food into his run. Jody was later able to confirm these details. I told Jody that I thought Dodger could change. When I talked with him, I did not get the feeling that he was determined to be vicious to humans. Instead, I felt that he was scared, confused, and extremely depressed. I made several suggestions to Jody, including that she talk to Dodger out loud and explain the situation to him. I told her to tell him what she hoped for from him and how he would have to behave if he wanted to live with her and Mike. I also told her to tell Dodger what would happen if he could not change his behavior. I told her to sit near his cage, close her eyes, and send love to him from her heart. I also told her to sing to him. There were many more suggestions, all geared toward shifting his behavior.

I also recommended that she change his name. My feeling was that his old name was so closely associated with his bad past experiences that he reacted adversely whenever he heard it. I recommend that people change an animal's name whenever there is negative emotional baggage attached to a name. To find a new name, I tell people to try out names that express the rescued animal's potential — who the animal could be given the right circumstances. Here is what Jody wrote about the outcome:

> After receiving your suggestions, we came up with the name Tasman and changed the dog's name right away. I talked to him and told him that we were giving him another chance, and I imagined sending love from my heart to his heart as you suggested. There was an immediate shift in his behavior. First he got very depressed — probably just a natural emotional progression as he slowed down from being frantic about his move — and then, finally, he was willing to make eye contact with me. Within days, he went from being terrifying to being a dog who smiled from ear to ear. Because of his past, he does have issues with women, and there are some things I just don't try — like patting him after feeding him, or touching him over or through a fence. I trust him now, though. When he sees me, he's joyful and runs to greet me. He absolutely loves the name Tasman. He also loves my husband. Mike can wrestle and play with him or brush and

massage him and Tasman loves it. Tasman will stay with us for life.

Often when I work with rescued or shelter animals, the person who calls me knows a little bit about the animal — a snippet of information written on the shelter adoption card, or some fact about the animal that got passed along in some way. Whenever I am asked to explore an animal's past, I advise people not to tell me anything they may already know. Then I can compare my results with the information they have. The more our information matches, the more confident we can be that my other findings are also accurate. Even if there is no information about an animal's past, intuitive information that comes in may be confirmed by the way the animal behaves. This was the case with Jet, Debbie Thompson's quarter-horse gelding. Debbie wrote:

> You said that you thought Jet might have been abused by a man with a mustache who wore a white T-shirt and a cowboy hat. I have seen Jet bolt several times when approached by guys at our barn who were wearing white T-shirts. To this day, he is skittish around men but unafraid of women.

Ali O'Neal sent this story about a consultation I did with her eight-year-old springer spaniel, Sammie:

> I adopted Sammie from a rescue organization about one year ago. You said that she told you she had belonged to an older woman, perhaps someone in her early sixties, and that the woman had received Sammie as a gift. You sensed that this woman adored the dog and that Sammie

was very happy there. Then you saw that the woman got very sick and died. After that, you felt that Sammie was passed on to family members who did not do so well with her, at which point she was placed at the animal shelter and adopted by the rescue group, which is where we met her.

Soon after that communication, we noticed that while out walking, Sammie always went up to older women and peered into their faces. It was if she were saying, "Are you my mama?" I had the paperwork from the family who took her to the shelter, and finally worked up the courage to call. I got a call back from the son of Sammie's previous person. Indeed, his mother died when she was sixty-two, and Sammie was the light of her life. The son had purchased Sammie when she was seven weeks old and given her to his mother as a gift. I did not question why he took her to the shelter, as it seemed to be a touchy issue. The son was overjoyed that Sammie's story had a happy ending.

We are now more sensitive to Sammie and to what she has gone through. We have two older women friends who adore Sammie and who often take her for walks. Sammie now has two women friends in her life who she knows better than we do, and she is very happy! You were also right about what area in Northern California she was from.

CHECKING ON PAST LIVES

Some clients call me to check on an animal's past, but they mean past lifetimes, not past experiences in this lifetime. A lot of people believe that animals reincarnate and that the animals in our lives have been with us in other forms and at other times. When I started out in this field, I had no opinion about the subject of reincarnation. I was raised a Unitarian and, basically, Unitarians believe in peace and potlucks. So I had no preconceptions or opinions about religious issues. In talking with the animals over the years, however, I have become convinced that they do reincarnate. If this idea is incredible to you, or if it goes against your religious beliefs, you can skip this discussion, go to the next section, and forget that I even mentioned the idea. There is no way for me to prove to you that reincarnation occurs, and I wouldn't even try. You do not have to believe in reincarnation in order to communicate intuitively with animals.

For myself, however, I've concluded based on my conversations with animals that they can reincarnate. Moreover, I feel that they can come back as either animals or people. Often when I ask an animal about its past lives with a particular person, I get a response like, "I was her son in human form," or, "We were wolves [or birds, or cats] together." This has happened so often that I no longer question it.

I also believe that the animals in our lives have been with us many times before, as have the people we are close to. What convinced me of this was the following incident with my current dog, Brydie, with whom you worked in the exercises in chapter 6. I got Brydie from the animal shelter as a five-month-old puppy. I selected her because I wanted a small black female dog to keep me and my other dog company. When I brought her home, she began to exhibit an odd behavior: At any opportunity, she would get behind me, jump up on my back, put her paws around my neck, and lick my ear.

Every time she did this, I immediately recalled something that had happened twelve years before. I was at a veterinary clinic, where I'd had to euthanize my elderly dog, Maka. I came out of the clinic and got into my car. As I sat there, I got a visual image of Maka as a puppy. In this image, which was almost like a movie, she was sitting on my shoulder and licking my ear from behind. At the time, I thought she was just saying good-bye and showing me herself as a puppy. I'd gotten her as an adult and had never seen her as a puppy. When Brydie kept repeating this licking behavior, I began to wonder if she were actually Maka.

I was so close to the situation that I did not have enough objectivity to ask her myself, so I called one of my colleagues and had her ask Brydie if she were really Maka. My colleague called back and said, "Yes she is, and she is wondering why it took you so long to figure it out!" As soon as I got that phone call, the behavior stopped; Brydie has never repeated it.

Clients often ask whether their animals have been with them before. When I check this out with the animal, I sometimes receive an image or get the name of a childhood pet — a pony named Daisy or a grey cat named Fred. From these experiences, I have concluded that many of our animals decide to come back to live with us. Not only that, but I believe that we don't have to do anything to find them. They simply work things out so that they find us.

The basic technique for asking whether an animal has been with you before in another body in this lifetime is the same as for all intuitive work: Ask, and then follow what comes in. You can also ask an animal to tell you about her past lifetimes. When you ask about past lives, you may receive a single image, feeling, or phrase that relates to a past lifetime. It might be something as vague as an image of a boat on an ocean. Your job then is to keep asking questions that will help you reveal the details and the importance of this image. With a boat image, you might ask questions like "Where and when is this? Who are you on this boat? Is your person there, too?" Usually, you won't be able to verify any-thing you get when you ask about past lives, so when you're prac-ticing you should just treat this as an interesting exercise.

THE ANIMALS IN OUR LIVES

Now that you have had some practice listening to your animals, you should be having two-way conversations with them. At this point you may want to try having a more in-depth discussion with your animal about any behavior problems she is exhibiting. When you do this, ask her to tell you why she's engaging in the problem behavior and what is needed to stop it.

Using the skill of hearing your animal intuitively, you can now ask things you may have long wondered about. If you sense a special connection with your animal, you can ask what that is about. You can find out why you two are together and ask her opinion of the choices you've made for her. The following sections will help you explore those issues.

Our Animals' Purpose in Our Lives

I believe that animals who end up in close connection with us are our teachers and spiritual partners. They show us how to love unconditionally — the same way they do. They teach us how to be totally connected with nature and present in the moment, as they are. Sometimes they have an additional special purpose in our lives. I know that my horse, Dylan, came to teach me how to help other horses. And my cat Jennifer is my master teacher of intuitive communication. Now that you can hear your animal, you can ask what special purpose she has for choosing to be with you.

Is It the Right Name?

Over the years, I have worked with animals who were saddled with some pretty bad names: Trouble, Danger, Dummy, Stinky, Craven, Jolt, Killer, Stud, Ice Cream, and Wimpy. I could go on. I never fail to be amazed when people tell me that they hate their animal's name and did not choose it, but have not changed it because they are worried that the animal won't be able to adjust to a new name — as if the animal will be lost and won't know who she is.

I hope that you understand by now that all you have to do is talk out loud to your animal and explain things, and your animal will understand perfectly. I have yet to meet an animal with a silly name who was unwilling to exchange it for a nice one. When an animal comes from an abusive or unpleasant situation, one of the best things you can do is to change her name; this immediately and dramatically helps the animal begin to heal.

If you're dealing with an animal behavior problem, changing the animal's name is an easy, free, and reversible experiment that can't hurt and might help. I have found it to be amazingly effective for my clients and myself. My orange kitty Chi, who used to fight a lot, told me that he hated his name and wanted to be called Marmalade. I resisted for a time because there's just no way to shorten that name; it's Marmalade or nothing. But when I finally gave in and changed it, he became a much sweeter, less combative cat.

Of course, you should ask first if your animal is happy with her current name; if so, keep it. If not, ask what she would like to be named. If the animal does not have a preference, come up with some names yourself and check them out with the animal. Take your time and search for names that best express the highest potential of the animal. Make a list and think about it for a while before you decide to try out a new name.

I Want a New Job!

Animals like to feel useful, just as humans do. If an animal is having behavioral problems, you should of course find out what may be physically wrong or whether there is anything upsetting in the environment. If those investigations lead nowhere, it is useful to try giving the animal some new tasks to do.

The animals we live with perform a number of jobs without even being asked. They guard us, comfort us, and entertain us. Often, in a house full of animals, you will notice that one animal acts as the peacemaker. Another may act as a teacher for the young or for new animals. Another may be the official greeter, and so on. Typically, these are jobs the animals have assumed on their own. You can also give animals specific jobs, and you may already have done this in your home. The jobs you give could range from the practical to the more emotional or spiritual. Here are some examples:

- Meet and greet you when you come home
- Make you go outside and exercise
- Watch out for the other animals in your home and warn you of any problems
- Give you advice
- Help you with your projects
- Help you with a problem you are having with a person or situation in your life (but make it clear that the animal is to stay happy and healthy, too, and to avoid taking on anything negative for you)

My cat Hazel helps me write; she is my muse. She is always there at my side when I sit down in front of the computer. My dog Bear is my protector, and he also helps me clean the house; he stays right by my side throughout vacuuming and mopping and makes the whole process fun. I tell them both how much I appreciate their help.

When you assign a new job to your animal, be sure to write it down and post it where you can see and be reminded of it. Observe whether your animal is doing the new job. If you see any signs that she is, be sure to give effusive praise; we all like to be appreciated for doing a good job. Also, be sure to reward and praise your animals for the jobs they are already doing for you. Check with your animals to find out what jobs they are doing now and whether they are happy with their current jobs. If not, change them.

The Problem of Mirroring

In his book, *The Nature of Animal Healing*,[1] veterinarian Dr. Martin Goldstein discusses a phenomenon he calls "resonance." In his practice, Goldstein observed a high incidence of animals that had illnesses and injuries identical to those of the people they lived with. He speculated that this phenomenon could occur because of animals' heightened empathic tendencies. Another possibility he considered is that the animals are trying to help their people by holding up a mirror to expose any disease and disharmony present in the human.

Most animals are so open and loving that they don't put up any barriers between themselves and people. They become like sponges, absorbing our energy. For example, they may become aggressive with people if we harbor fear or hostility toward others, or they may get depressed when we are. When they do this, they are acting like a mirror showing us that we are out of balance emotionally and giving us an opportunity to correct the imbalance.

They may do this on purpose, as a helpful gesture, or they may do it inadvertently as a result of being enmeshed with our emotions.

Animals also often mimic our diseases. Take a close look at your animal's health problems. If you suspect that your animal is mirroring your health problems, have a talk with her about it. Explain that you appreciate it if she is doing this to help you, but that you want her to be healthy and happy. Ask her instead to be a model of health and happiness for you to follow.

If you feel that your animal is mirroring something negative in you, be it a behavior or an illness, have a talk with her and tell her what you would rather she do. Then work on yourself to change your poor behavior or improve your health. This will often eliminate the corresponding problems in your animal.

LOOKING INTO THE FUTURE

If you can use your intuition to look into the past, then you should also be able to use it to look into the future. I do this for people when they are considering adopting a new animal. I imagine the animal with the person or in the home with the existing animals at some point in the future — say two weeks ahead — to see what the outcome will be. So far, I have been pretty accurate and the process has been helpful for my clients.

I haven't been as successful in predicting whether a pregnant animal is going to have male or female offspring. And I wouldn't even try to use intuition to bet on horses because I don't support that industry. But there are many times when it's handy to at least get a sense of a future outcome. For example, a friend called me recently, upset because her horse was lame and the veterinarians who had seen the horse were saying that the horse would be lame for life. When I looked six weeks into the future, I saw her horse recovered and I saw her riding the horse again. Within about a week, her horse was almost completely recovered and a second opinion from another veterinarian indicated that the horse would be fine.

The main technique for looking ahead is to imagine a future situation or event. Observe it as if you are watching a movie and see what images, feelings, or words come through. You could also ask for information to be transmitted to you from universal knowledge and then record whatever comes in.

EXERCISES: PAST, PRESENT, AND FUTURE

These exercises will give you practice in everything that was covered in this chapter. You can do them with your own animals or with a friend's animals. Choose whichever focusing and connecting methods work best for you (the methods are summarized on pages 129–130 in chapter 8). You can work with your eyes open or closed, whichever is more comfortable for you. Use a deep breath as your cue whenever you want to feel focused, relaxed, and open to your intuition. Remember to record all your results in your notebook.

Exercise 1: Checking an Animal's Past Experiences

Ask the animal to show or tell you what happened to her in the past. If you get something vague — such as an image of a backyard — ask for more information: What did the backyard look like? Did she have to stay there all the time? Did she get to go indoors? Did she go on walks? Let's say you get a feeling that she was with a family. Then ask her how many people there were, what their ages were, and what they looked like. Ask how she felt when she was living there. If you persist and ask the right questions, you should be able to get a good idea of what her past was like.

Exercise 2: Exploring an Animal's Past Lives

Ask the animal to show or tell you about whether she has been with her person before in this lifetime. As you get impressions — images, feelings, or words — ask the animal to expand upon and explain the information. Ask for names and descriptions of what animals she may have been. Then ask her about her past lifetimes. As you get an impression of another lifetime, record the information and ask the animal to give more details. Find out what the animal was in that lifetime — possibly another animal species or a human. Ask what was important about that lifetime and find out what beliefs the animal held and what decisions she made based on her experiences in that lifetime. If you are working with your own animal, ask for the details of any relationship you and she may have had in that lifetime.

Exercise 3: Do You Like Your Name?

Ask the animal whether she likes her name. If not, ask why and ask what name she would like. If she does like her name, ask her why she likes it.

Exercise 4: Do You Like Your Job?

Ask the animal what her jobs are now. Find out whether she likes those jobs. If not, ask why and find out what jobs she would like to do. You may also suggest some jobs you would like her to do and see if they appeal to her.

Exercise 5: Mirroring

Ask the animal whether she is mirroring a physical or emotional condition for you (or for her person). If so, have a discussion about this. Tell the animal that your wish is for her to be as happy and healthy as possible. Explain that you would like her to stop mirroring and instead be a model of health and happiness. Then work on changing your unwanted behavior or improving your health (or suggest that the animal's person do so), as this will probably benefit the animal.

Exercise 6: Looking into the Future

Imagine a future situation involving the animal — for example, an upcoming show, a ride on a new trail, or a visit to a new veterinarian. Observe this future event as if you were there or watching a movie of it. Record any images, feelings, or words that come through. You might also want to ask universal knowledge how this event will play out in the future. Then record whatever comes in.

Chapter Twelve

In Sickness and in Health

An animal communicator is often the last resort for people who have a sick or injured animal and have tried everything, although, as more people learn about this field, communicators are being called in to help sooner. Intuitive work can reveal information that may prove valuable to the animal's recovery. Being able to communicate directly with the animal is also helpful to people who are facing the moral dilemma of whether and when to put down a fatally injured or terminally ill animal. And contacting the spirit of an animal after death can ease people's grief.

Debbie Thompson, a client of mine, recounts an experience that illustrates the role of intuitive work in solving a perplexing health problem:

> Early in 1999, my quarter-horse gelding, Jet, started having pretty bad behavior problems such as kicking at people,

running away from me, and biting. At that same time, he came down with a pretty severe lameness in his left front leg. I called vet after vet and got a different diagnosis each time: navicular disease, shoulder injury, or just bad attitude because I was letting him get away with too much. This went on for weeks, and the behavior continued to be bad. I would treat him with a painkiller, as the vets recommended, but he would improve only a little bit. I was so frustrated that I decided to call you when I saw your name in a journal article.

You said that you felt that the source of his pain was in his hoof, and you also felt that there was a nail or something metal stuck up in his hoof that was irritating him. I had the farrier come out, and he discovered an abscess in Jet's foot that had gone undiagnosed by two vets. I then had a third vet come out who pulled a metal fragment out of Jet's hoof! By then his general health had somewhat declined from the effects of this long-standing infection, and his behavior was still bad. Over time, you have helped me with advice and resources for getting Jet healthy and happy again. He is doing fine now.

In this chapter, I will explain the process of medical intuition and energy healing. I will also tell you what I have learned about how to keep my animals healthy and how to assist animals when they are dying. At the end of the chapter, you can try your hand at some exercises in medical intuition and communication with sick or injured animals.

Medical Intuition

Medical intuition — gaining intuitive insight into the well-being of an individual — can be performed on animals as well as people. When working with animals, I ask the animal about his health, much as a physician would interview a human patient. While the results can be very accurate, medical intuition should never be used as a diagnostic tool because there is always the possibility of error in intuitive work. I consider my results to be completely speculative unless they can be verified. Before I agree to work with a sick or injured animal, I require that the animal first be evaluated by a professional animal caregiver.

Medical intuition goes beyond conventional medical practice to explore the potential emotional, mental, and spiritual aspects of illness and injury. Physical problems will sometimes clear up after a change in life circumstances or the resolution of an emotional problem.

The Process

A medical intuitive session with an animal is much the same as a more general intuitive communication session, except that you need to be careful not to take on any of the pain or discomfort the animal is feeling. You should also know how to release any such energies if you do inadvertently absorb them. In this chapter, I will teach you techniques both for avoiding taking on the animal's condition and for clearing out anything you may inadvertently absorb.

I get concerned when I see an animal communicator do something like grabbing her own back and saying, "Oh, your animal has a horrible pain in his back. I can feel it right here." There's no need to actually feel an animal's pain in order to be able to identify it, and it isn't a healthy thing to do; it doesn't help the animal get better, and it can make you feel ill. It is possible to determine what's going on in an animal's body — even to get a sense of a what the animal is feeling — without having to bring it into your own body. The technique is simple: Clearly set your intention not to take on any pain, disease, or emotion from the animals you work with. This does take some practice, but it works.

Sometimes, though, you may accidentally pick up some negative energy from an animal. This can happen when you first start practicing, of course, but no matter how accomplished and vigilant you become, it can still happen, because humans are as empathic as other animals. If you were ever around an animal who was very sad you may recall how hard it was not to feel exactly as that animal felt.

Here's what to do if you do take on an animal's symptoms. This technique works for releasing both emotional and physical pain that you might inadvertently assimilate. Let's say you are talking with an animal who has been refusing to eat, and your stomach starts to hurt or you start to feel sick. If that happens, treat the sensation as if it were a residue that got attached to your body. Use your hands to "pull" and "wipe" this sensation from your body and flick it downward to the ground. Do this until you feel the sensation subside. When you send the energy into the ground, do so with the thought that it will be recycled by the earth and turned into useful energy again, just like composting. Then continue your conversation with a renewed intention to clearly receive information, but not to take on the animal's discomfort.

Interviewing a Sick or Injured Animal

When I work with a sick or injured animal, I always start out by asking the animal to tell me what his symptoms are and where he has discomfort in his body. Then I ask him if he can tell me what's causing his problems and what he thinks is wrong. I ask him to go into detail about his past illnesses and any injuries or life events that may be contributing to his ill health. Of course, I view all the information I get through this process as purely speculative. Some of it can be verified immediately if the animal's person knows the animal's medical history and record of injuries. Other information will have to be verified by a professional animal caregiver. Medical intuitive information should always be treated as speculative unless it can be verified in some way.

Exploring the Emotion behind Illness

In my experience, many common diseases and injuries of domestic animals are caused by an unhealthy environment and/or inadequate care and handling practices. I believe that holistic health care, a nontoxic environment, and an organic whole-food diet, combined with positive, nonviolent training methods, can resolve or eliminate a huge number of the problems that we have been resigned to accepting as part of our animals' lives.[1] However, it is always useful to look for underlying emotional causes when confronted with disease or injury in an animal. Stress or even a past trauma may very well be the underlying cause of an animal's physical illness and injury. An animal may also become ill because he is mirroring an emotion, behavior, illness, or injury he is picking up from his person. In these cases, it is good to talk things through.

If you are working with a sick or injured animal, you should explore these issues and find out what the animal can tell you about his life circumstances or emotional states. You should also try to determine whether the animal is mirroring anything from his people and, if so, find out why. I also like to follow up by asking universal knowledge for additional information about the animal's condition. And finally, I ask the animal what he believes he needs in order to heal.

Scanning an Animal's Body

Energy continually animates the physical body. Using intuition, it's possible to scan an animal's body and get impressions about the animal's health and well-being based on the energy in the animal's body. The body-scanning technique I recommend involves using your hands. You can do this in person or at a distance. If you have the animal right there, start at the animal's head and slowly move your hands along the body without touching it. Basically, you are feeling the energy in the animal's body. It helps to close your eyes when you do this. Become aware of places in the animal's body that don't feel "right." You may get a sense of cold or hot, or you may find that your hand just stops at a certain point. You may feel something rough or hard or weak as you move your hand along. If you pay attention, you should be able to detect some variations in the energy of the animal's body with your hands.

As soon as you detect anything or feel that you have located a problem area in the animal's body, stop and ask the animal what he feels in this area and whether he has any symptoms of disease or injury there. If you can't get anything detailed from the animal, remember that you can always fall back on the indirect questioning method and ask the universe what's wrong. As always, it is crucial to record any impressions that come to you. I usually note the problem areas I find by jotting them down on a sketch I've drawn of the animal.

The technique for body scanning is the same when you work with an animal at a distance, except that in this case you will have to imagine that the animal is there in front of you and then proceed to perform the body scan with your hands. When I do this, I often "shrink" the animal down to a more manageable size to be able to stay seated and work with the image of the animal at my desk. So if I am working with a horse, the experience is like scanning a small figurine of a horse.

Sometimes I use a different technique to scan an animal, in place of or in addition to the hand scanning. I imagine becoming the animal and being inside the animal's body. Before doing this technique, I renew my intention not to take on any symptoms from the animal, because in doing this I will have a more direct awareness of what an animal is feeling. This technique is useful when, for whatever reason, the hand-scanning process does not reveal sufficient information.

Let's take a case I worked on recently, involving a horse who refused to turn to the right for no discernable reason. I worked with this horse from a distance, so I just imagined him in front of me. When I scanned the horse's body, the information I received was vague, so I switched to the technique of imagining being the horse. To do this, I closed my eyes and imagined that I was inside the horse's body. From this perspective, I was able to sense what the horse felt. I imagined turning to the right, at which point I became aware that the horse experienced a huge jolt of pain in his right shoulder. I also become aware of the saddle pressing into the horse's shoulder. Based on this awareness, I concluded that the horse might have a problem with the saddle. I perceived the sensations the horse was feeling, but I did not take them on.

I advised the woman to have her horse evaluated by an equine bodyworker and to get her saddle checked by an expert saddle fitter. The bodyworker confirmed that there was soreness in the horse's right shoulder, and the saddle fitter advised the woman to get a different saddle for her horse. Once she changed the saddle, the horse had no more difficulties.

Some of my students meet regularly in groups to practice medical intuition. One such group told me of an older horse they worked with, using the interviewing and body-scanning techniques described above. There were ten people in the group, working from a photograph of the horse. When they finished, they compared notes. Each person had received a complaint from the horse about a different body part. They decided that one or two of them might have been right, but that the rest must have bombed. They called the horse's person to find out which answers were correct, and discovered that the horse was generally rundown and actually had all ten of the maladies that he had reported!

Energy Clearing

When you finish doing the body scan, it's a good idea to clear your energy field even if you didn't feel the animal's symptoms — just to make sure you don't absorb anything harmful. You can do this by pulling any unwanted energy from your body and sending it into the earth for recycling, as I described previously.

ENERGY HEALING

"Energy healing" means directing energy to promote healing and well-being. I believe that everyone can heal with energy, just as everyone can communicate intuitively; we are born being able to do this. Everyone has healing hands, but we don't always know this about ourselves. Essentially, any technique that results in healing in the body involves balancing and strengthening energy. In my experience, resting, physical therapy, exercise, herbs, homeopathy, acupuncture, other alternative treatments and selected conventional medicines and treatments have the effect of creating more balance and strength in the body. When your energy is balanced and strong, you are in optimum health. However, the term "energy healing" has come to be associated exclusively with the practice of purposely directing healing energy to another. This can be done with one's hands on the body, or with the hands removed from the surface of the body, and even at a distance, in the same way that intuitive communication can be done at a distance.

Purposely directing energy for healing is similar to using thought and prayer to heal. Physician Larry Dossey has written extensively about the power of the mind in the healing process.[2] He has conducted scientific studies that demonstrate the phenomenon of healing through prayer.

"Reiki" (pronounced "ray-kee") is one of the better known energy-healing techniques. Reiki was developed in Japan and is now taught throughout the world. It is helpful to study techniques like Reiki to learn how to fine-tune your healing ability, but you can start experimenting with energy healing on your own right now.

How to Heal with Energy

I will describe a simple method for healing with energy. (At the end of this chapter, I will summarize this technique and give you some exercises in energy healing to try on your own.) Before you start, make sure that the animal you are working with wants an energy healing session.

In energy healing, you will access the healing energy located at the core of the earth and in the vast universe above. Imagine this healing energy coming into you from the earth and the universe. You can close your eyes and feel the energy flowing, or you might imagine it as a color — for example, a golden light — coming into you from the ground and from above your head. Once you have tapped into these energies, direct them through your body and out through the palms of your hands toward the animal who needs healing. When you are present with the animal, you can place your hands directly on the animal or you can stand or sit a few feet away and hold your palms facing the animal, focusing on the parts of the animal that need healing. If you are working from a distance, you can close your eyes, imagine the animal is in front of you, and hold your palms facing that image of the animal.

Your role as an energy healer is simply to direct healing energy coming from the earth and the universe to the animal. You are not using your own energy to heal the animal, and therefore you will not run the risk of depleting yourself.

The medical intuitive session that you did with the animal should give you an idea of where the animal needs energy. You can send energy to all parts of the animal's body, focusing on those areas that feel the weakest. As you send energy, you may feel your palms warming up. Then, as the animal takes in the energy, you may feel your palms cool off. Do not force this process. Just let the energy be there and let the animal take what he needs. Be very gentle, as animals are much more sensitive than people. You don't have to do much; just make the energy available. Don't feel that you have to direct or understand the entire process; the energy from the earth and the universe will go where it is needed. Sometimes all I do is to imagine opening up the flow of energy and then ask that the animal receive whatever he needs. You may, however, find yourself drawn to parts of the animal's body that feel congested or blocked. You might feel this as cold or rough areas as your hands hover above the body. In these areas, you can pull the blocked energy out of the animal's body and then flick it down to the earth to be recycled.

At the end of the energy-healing session, I always send some additional energy with the intention that whatever the animal needs for his healing is brought to him. I ask that whatever supplements, medical practitioners, bodyworkers, or changed life circumstances the animal needs in order to become healthy and happy be sent to him by the universe. You can send the healing energy for as long as it feels right to you. You should feel a shift when you have sent enough energy. You might feel the energy flow slowing or stopping. You might just get the message intuitively from universal knowledge that you have sent enough. When you feel that you are finished, end by sending love. Then clear your own energy as previously described in this chapter. You can also go wash your hands as a way of formally clearing your energy.

Energy healing can be remarkably effective, and it can help with emotional problems as well as physical ones. Whenever I work with an animal who is upset, I always do energy healing — even when I'm working at a distance. I recently did this with Steve and Rachael Adler's cat, Norman, who had retreated under the bed after the Adlers had a new baby and was only coming out to eat. This behavior had been going on for weeks. Norman had experienced behavior problems in the past, which had been resolved through my communication with him and the Adlers' use of alternative holistic therapies. But this time he wasn't responding to anything.

In desperation, I did an extended long-distance energy-healing session with him. I directed healing energy to the image of Norman, as if he were right in front of me. I concentrated on releasing the strong emotions I could feel as blocked energy in his body. I sent him feelings of love and worked to balance his energy. After the session, he came out of hiding. At last report, he was staying out, moving about, and even greeting people at the door — a new and welcome behavior in a cat who was previously afraid of strangers.

HAVING HEALTHY ANIMALS

In the majority of my consultations, I end up referring people to holistic health-care resources and practitioners. I do this because many of the problems people call me about have nothing to do with their animal's emotions or with what's going on in the home. The problems are more related to physical problems, care, and nutrition issues. I advise people to seek out a holistic veterinarian to care for their animals (see resources). A holistic veterinarian will balance the use of traditional medicine with alternative therapies such as acupuncture, chiropractic, and massage, and will complement traditional pharmaceuticals with herbs, nutrition, and homeopathic remedies. The holistic veterinarian can also evaluate which vaccines an animal needs and how often. Most holistic veterinarians believe that we tend to give animals too many vaccines.[3] The holistic veterinarians can also advise about the use of homeopathy to help offset the negative effects of vaccines.

A holistic veterinarian can assist people in diminishing or eliminating the use of toxic chemicals for their animals, including those used for the control of fleas, flies, ticks, and internal parasites. It is especially important to protect animals from exposure to pesticides or other poisons in the environment. This includes exposure to agricultural chemicals used on crops adjacent to the stable or property, and possible toxins that may be in the groundwater.[4]

Finally, the holistic veterinarian can devise a natural, whole-food diet for an animal. I have found that my animals do best when fed organically grown foods — free from pesticides and genetic engineering. (You should be eating that way, too!) I do feed my animals raw meat, and I try to ensure that it comes from animals who were raised as humanely as possible. Usually, you can only find this at a natural food store. I try to stay current on issues of holistic health for animals by searching the Internet and reading journals and books on the subject.

Specific Recommendations for Dogs and Cats

After I started feeding my dogs and cats natural whole foods instead of commercial foods, about seven years ago, I noticed an incredible improvement in their health. Many people are now feeling their dogs and cats a "raw food" diet or the "BARF" diet (Bones And Raw Food). I have seen such diets work miracles, and I highly recommend them. To find out how to provide animals with whole food, check the suggested reading and resources sections at the end of this book. If people can't take the time to feed animals whole foods, I stress the importance of buying the top-end commercial foods — those that do not contain meat byproducts.[5] You can verify this by reading the food labels.

Some of my clients who are vegetarian feed their dogs a whole-food diet that does not include meat and bones. I think you can do this with dogs if you are careful and do good research,[6] but I am not convinced that cats can live on a vegetarian diet. One solution for vegetarians would be to only have pets who are naturally vegetarian, such as rabbits, horses, goats, and birds. That would eliminate the moral issue of killing animals for meat.[7]

Specific Recommendations for Horses

In selecting feed for horses, natural-care advocates suggest limiting the use of alfalfa hay or pellets; problems with behavior, performance, kidneys, and colic have been linked to overfeeding alfalfa to horses.[8] It's also a good idea to avoid giving a horse sugar or any artificial preservatives (read the ingredients of the feed). My alternative equine veterinarian recommended that I use a probiotic on my horse to enhance his digestion. A probiotic supplement contains the beneficial bacteria needed for efficient digestion of food (e.g., acidophilous), and can be purchased at most feed stores.

Make sure a horse always has plenty of water. The small automatic waterers don't allow the horse to take enough water at one time — and if the power goes off, the horse might go without water, which can lead to colic. A few big secure buckets or a bathtub, refilled daily, are the best way to provide water. In winter, the water needs to be kept from freezing, or the ice in the horse's trough needs to be broken regularly.

A horse should also have his teeth checked yearly. I have had the best results from using an equine dentist for this, as these individuals have specialized knowledge and skills. Improper tooth care or a lack of care can make it difficult for the horse to chew food well enough to absorb nutrients. It can also cause severe muscle pain, displaced vertebrae, and aggression or other unwanted behaviors in the horse.

Whenever there is a problem with lameness, check the shoeing. Finding a good shoer is not easy; it may require shopping around. In addition to calling in the veterinarian, it is also helpful to consult with an equine bodyworker and a chiropractor in cases of lameness.

If a horse acts oddly when saddled, it is likely that the saddle does not fit properly. An expert saddle fitter should evaluate the saddle. A good saddle is hard to find, so this process may take time. If a horse acts badly when ridden, it is probably the saddle, the bridle or bit, his teeth, his bones or muscles, or the rider's technique. So start anywhere you like, but don't give up until you find the problem — and don't let a trainer advise that the horse be gotten rid of.

HELPING A DYING ANIMAL

Animals do not have the same attitude about death that we do. They don't relate to death as alarming or final. They are more aware of the world of the spirit than we are, and they know that the spirit never dies. For animals, death just isn't the kind of ending that it is for us.

When I talk with dying animals, I find that they often want assistance with dying in order to avoid pain. This was the case with Duke, an elderly horse with severe hoof problems. His person was dying of cancer, and Sara Hartman was trying to help out by taking care of Duke. She tried several treatments to help him recover, but was unable to control his problem. Duke and Sara had a good relationship; he always seemed happy to see her and appeared to enjoy her company. But, Sara suspected that Duke might be so uncomfortable that he would not want to continue living, and she called me to find out if this was true. When I talked with him, Duke said that he had headaches and pain with every step and that he was unable to sleep. He said that he was ready to go, and that he was sad to be so helpless and in so much pain. Sara corroborated the fact that he was barely able to move, and that he had lost his interest in life. Without hesitation, she made the necessary arrangements to have the veterinarian end Duke's life.

Although they are not afraid to die, dying animals still grieve over having to leave this life. They know that their experience of this life can never be repeated, and the relationships forged are unique. When an animal dies, the surviving animals in the household and other animal friends may become just as emotionally devastated as the grieving people. While they do have the awareness that their friend can return, they also know when he does that he will not be the same and he might not return for some time.

Preparing for Death

Here are some things you can do to make the transition from physical form to the spiritual form easier for both an animal and those who love him. (You can pass on this list to anyone you know who is in this situation.):

- Ask your animal to give you a clear sign if he wants to be assisted in dying.
- Tell your animal all the things you have learned from him and all the reasons you are grateful he came into your life.
- Make a book of memories, poems, and photographs of your animal.
- Make an altar for your animal.
- Decide how you will treat the body (burial, cremation).[9]
- Have a good-bye party with all the animal's friends (make it happy!).
- Sit with your animal with your eyes closed and feel his energy so that you will be able to recognize that energy once your animal goes into the spirit.

- Tell your animal if you would like him to come back into your life in another body.

When Is the Right Time?

You can use intuitive communication to check in with a dying animal and find out whether he wants help with the dying process. However, the information you get may be surprising. Some animals who look like they're ready to go will tell you that they plan to hold on a while longer because they want to stay with their people until the very end. Miraculously, some might even recover from death's door and go on to live another year or more. Others will tell you that they are more than ready to go and want help. Some will say they can't leave until their people are more comfortable with their death. I try never to prejudge the situation, and instead work to hear objectively what the animal wants. If an animal is ready to go and wants help with dying, it is easier for the animal once his person can hear and accept this. Jenny Watson sent me this story about her experience of putting down her older retired horse, Gomer:

> Gomer was the love of my life. I felt toward him like a mother feels toward a child. He was very trusting and always tried hard for me. He was extremely successful in the show ring, winning numerous championships and year-end awards. Right before Thanksgiving, he went off his feed and started lying down. That was the beginning of a four-week stretch that came to an end with Gomer's death. I had the vet come out ten times that first week, feeding Gomer fluids and electrolytes via a tube and trying different supplements and medications. Nothing

really helped, but at least the fluids kept him hydrated. He never totally regained his appetite, but he seemed happy when I came out; he ate carrots for me and enjoyed walking down the road a bit. I had been afraid to even pull his blanket off for some time — afraid to see how much weight he might have lost. Finally, almost a month later, I decided that the next time I went out to see him I'd pull off his blanket and take an objective look at the situation.

On my next visit, I brought him into the barn and took off his blanket. While he wasn't dangerously thin, he looked tired and run down. After all those weeks, I finally let myself cry because I knew in my heart that I had to let him go. When I started to cry and leaned my head against his neck, he turned to look at me. What I saw in his eyes was, "It's OK." The next day was a Friday. I called the vet and made the appointment for Monday. I came out to see Gomer each of those last days. He was lying down a lot of the time, so I'd sit either on a bucket at his head or on the ground next to him and cry while I tried to get him to eat. He did eat a little for me each day, but I could tell he wasn't hungry; he was only trying to make me feel better.

On Monday, I arrived at the stable three hours ahead of the vet. I sat with Gomer and cried, told him how much I loved him, and thanked him for everything he'd done for me. I also kept saying that I didn't know what I was going to do without him, how I'd manage. I told him that the vet would be coming in a few hours and that I needed him to be brave because I wouldn't be. All that time, he looked at me knowingly, in the best way he could, telling me, "It's OK." At one point, he got up and walked over to an adjoining paddock where there was a horse he used to be turned out with. They looked at each other without touching — just stared at each other — and then Gomer walked back over to me. I'm pretty sure Gomer was saying good-bye. They weren't upset; they just seemed to know. Then he walked up to me and I patted his forehead while I cried, telling him again how much I loved him and asking him if I was doing the right thing.

At that point, he picked up his head, gently set it on my shoulder, and softly blew his breath into my ear. Again, he looked at me as if to say, "It's OK." I told him that I'd brought some baggies with me because I wanted to cut off some of his mane and tail hair to keep with me. I pulled the blanket off his shoulder to cut some hair. Then, on his own, Gomer walked past me and backed his tail right up to me. That made me cry even more, but it also made me feel that he knew and understood exactly what I was saying and feeling, and that he was doing his best to help me through it.

When the vet came, Gomer again looked at me knowingly like he was at peace and ready to go. Putting Gomer to sleep was without a doubt the hardest thing I've ever had to do. As hard as those last few days were, knowing that all I had to do was call the vet and cancel the appointment, I have no regrets. My suspicion is that Gomer had abdominal tumors or something of that nature. I knew that he might very well have been able to live a bit longer, but I couldn't bear the thought that he might experience a painful ending or become debilitated. I was willing to give up some time with him for a guarantee that he wouldn't have to die in pain or suffering. I retired him from the show ring sound and winning, and I wanted him to have that dignity when he died, too.

It's a horrifying and terrifying feeling to have the power to dictate when another being lives or dies. It's much easier to wait until the choice is obvious, but that choice often comes with a price that is usually paid by the animal you love. I loved Gomer so much that I was willing to let him go, and in many, many ways he acknowledged that, told me that it was a good and correct thing to do, and did his best to tell me that he loved me, too.

Connecting with Animals after Death

I believe that animals stay close to us in spirit long after they've left their bodies. I think they do this to help us get through the experience. I know that when my dog Dougal died, I could feel his head on my knee and I would catch his scent on occasion. I felt his presence for a time whenever we did his favorite things — eating and walking. Clients have called with similar tales: catching a fleeting glimpse of the animal, finding an indentation on the bed where the animal used to sleep, or seeing muddy pawprints on the rug that faded upon inspection. All of these are messages to tell us that our animals are still with us in spirit, even though they had to leave their damaged, worn-out bodies.

My experience is that once we are able to function again after an animal's death, their spirits go elsewhere, but that they are always right there if we call on them or need them. The death of an animal can be as painful as losing a person in your life, if not more so. Animals give us true, uncomplicated love. To lose that does not feel good — ever. Being able to talk with them after death helps ease the pain, but grief over losing animals is an unavoidable part of sharing your life with them.

People who believe that animals reincarnate often call to find out whether an animal plans to come back into another body. When I communicate with animals who have died, some of them are not at all interested in coming back to the earth. They seem to have lots to do in the spirit realm and aren't ready to be in a body again. Other animals can't wait to come back. I feel very certain that if an animal wants to be with you again, he will find you; you don't have to do anything except pay attention to your intuitive feelings. If you get an uncanny feeling of connection with an animal, it is probably because that animal has been with you before. If you believe in reincarnation, simply tell your departed animal that you would love to have him come back if he wants to, and ask him to make it really obvious to you when he returns.

EXERCISES: IN SICKNESS AND HEALTH

The following exercises will give you practice in all the areas covered in this chapter. Choose whichever focusing and connecting methods work best for you (summarized in chapter 8, pages 129–130). You can work with your eyes open or closed, whichever is more comfortable. Use a deep breath as your cue whenever you want to feel focused, relaxed, and open to your intuition. Make sure to record all your results in your notebook.

Medical Intuition/Energy Healing

Exercise 1: Interview a Sick or Injured Animal

Ask the animal to show or tell you where he has discomfort in his body. Remember to record everything without censure. Now ask the animal to tell you about his history: what injuries and illnesses has he had? Record your results. Ask if there is anything going on that is affecting his health, and ask whether mirroring from his person is a factor.

Ask the animal if he knows what he needs in order to heal. Then ask universal knowledge for any additional information you may have overlooked about this animal. If you inadvertently picked up any unwanted energy from the animal, clear your body and flick the energy down to the earth for recycling. Do this until you feel any unwanted sensations subside.

It is important to realize that any information you get about the physical or emotional condition of an animal could be wrong. Everyone gets inaccurate information some of the time. You will have to be especially careful to emphasize this point when you convey your results to the animal's person. Don't ever assume that your results are accurate unless they've been verified. If you pick up something negative, explain that you have no idea whether it is correct. Tell the person that you would be interested in follow-up information about the animal. Let the animal's person be the final judge of whether your information is correct.

Exercise 2: Scan the Body

Ask the animal for permission to scan the body, and proceed if you receive it. Get out your notebook and make a rough sketch of the animal. The sketch can be about half the size of a piece of typing paper. Imagine that the animal is in front of you and connect with him. Starting at his head, use your hands to scan his body and feel whether there are any problem areas. If so, stop and make a note of the area on your sketch. Then ask the animal and the universe what's wrong in that area. Record your results. Continue until you have scanned the entire body.

Exercise 3: Send Healing Energy

Ask the animal for permission to send healing energy, and proceed if it seems all right. Imagine healing energy coming into you from the earth and the universe, then flowing through the palms of your hands. Imagine the animal in front of you and direct the energy toward the animal (again, you can do this whether the animal is near or far). As you send the energy, you may feel your palms warm up. Then, as the animal takes in the energy, you may feel your palms cool off. Do not force this. Just let the energy be there and let the animal take what he needs. Be very gentle; just make the energy available. You may find parts of the animal's body that feel congested or blocked. In these areas, pull energy out of the animal's body and then flick it down to the earth to be recycled.

When you feel that the session is complete, send some energy with the intention that whatever the animal needs in order to heal is brought to him: He receives whatever supplements, medical practitioners, bodyworkers, or changed life circumstances he needs in order to become healthy and happy. Now send love and clear your own energy as previously described. You can also go wash your hands as a way to clear your energy if you wish. Record any impressions from the session in your notebook.

Death and Dying

Exercise 4: Interview an Animal About Death

Ask an animal — your own or someone else's — to tell you how he feels about the subject of death. Is it something he worries about? What does he have to say on the subject?

Exercise 5: Interview a Dying Animal

If one of your friends has an animal who is dying, you might offer to help by talking with the animal. I have found this kind of communication to be extremely calming and reassuring to people. If your friend wants your help, get a list of any questions your friend has for the animal. Then ask the animal if he understands what's happening and ask how he feels about the situation. Ask him the questions supplied by your friend. Before you end the session, ask if he has anything else to say.

You can also do this same process with your own animal. It might be more difficult because of the grief and upset you may be feeling, but if you want to try it, go ahead.

Exercise 6: Talk with an Animal Who Has Died

You can try this exercise with one of your own animals from the past or with a friend's animal. If you don't believe in reincarnation, just eliminate the questions at the end that deal with that subject.

Connect with the animal's spirit. Ask the animal the following questions:

- How are you?
- What is it like where you are?
- Do you have any memories you want to share with me about your life?
- Is there anything you want to say?
- Are you still in the spirit, or are you in a new body?
- Are you planning to come back into a body? If so, can you tell me more about that?

Chapter Thirteen

Lost Animals

U sing intuitive communication to find lost animals is difficult. A lot of animal communicators prefer not to attempt it
because the results tend to be less accurate than for other types of
consultations. When people call about a lost animal, I let them
know that the results may be inconclusive. I also tell them that I
have helped lead people directly to their lost animals, so I know it
can be worth the gamble. But it is a gamble, so if funds are limited I advise people to invest in ads and flyers instead. I caution
that any information I provide about a lost animal must be treated
as conjecture unless it can be verified.

When an animal is lost, I recommend taking the following
actions at once:

- Post flyers in the neighborhood and within a one-
  mile radius of the animal's last known location.

- Talk to neighbors, children at local schools, delivery people, and workers in the area about the lost animal.
- Check the shelters, humane societies, pet supply stores, animal service businesses, and veterinary clinics in the area.
- Ask friends to pray for the animal's safe return. If you know any people who do energy healing, ask them to send energy for protection and the safe return of the animal.

The resources section in the back of this book lists Web sites that provide more detailed information about how to search for a lost animal, including names of businesses that will help with the search.

When I lost my cat Marmalade, I could think only of the horrible things that could be happening to him. That's not a good place to go. Instead, imagine reuniting with the lost animal and think of her as being safe and protected.

A person whose animal is lost may think that going to sleep is a waste of precious search time. But loss of sleep makes one an ineffective searcher. Instead, you can use sleep time to gather intuitive information about the lost animal. When you sleep, you are at your most intuitive; you can also access your intuition in your dreams. Before you go to bed, say out loud that you want to get information in your dreams that will help you find the animal. Then make sure that you have a pen and paper beside the bed. Set your alarm clock for about five minutes earlier than your usual rising time; waking up a little earlier helps you remember your dreams better. Before you get out of bed the next morning, record anything you remember from your dreams.

ACCURACY AND LOST-ANIMAL CASES

I have not done a scientific study of my accuracy rate with lost animals, but my rough assessment is that I am about 60 to 70 percent accurate in such cases. In my other work, I estimate that I am about 80 to 90 percent accurate. Based on the feedback I've received from clients, I tend to be right most of the time about whether the animal is dead or alive and about which direction and what distance to search in. But sometimes the details I get about what happened to the animal can be off. And sometimes, despite my best efforts, the animal is never found.

If more than one animal communicator is involved in a search, they may each come up with a different scenario. The best way to deal with this is to treat each piece of intuitive information as a possible piece of the puzzle to the lost animal's whereabouts. Investigate each puzzle piece and see where it leads. Until there is real proof, it is impossible to know what truly happened to the animal. Not knowing is the worst part of losing an animal.

Finding lost animals using intuition is so tricky that it is almost an art form. Lost-animal cases can also be highly emotional and nerve-wracking. In fact, there are so many negative factors in finding lost animals that I have considered not doing it any more. However, I now have over ten years of practice at it and I've had some good results. I hate to throw away all that experience. And success can lead to some wonderful reunions.

For example, a couple called about their cat who had escaped from the boarding kennel while they were on vacation. When I got in touch with the cat, he showed me his exact route, including direction, and his current location. As if in a movie, I retraced his steps: leaving the kennel, going north for two blocks, then west another two, and ending at a big gray warehouse adjacent to a mini-storage business and some railroad tracks. The couple followed the clues and found all the reference points. They found the warehouse, which was a commercial laundry. They also saw their cat, but he wouldn't come to them. They tried trapping him, sitting for hours at the warehouse, but the cat refused to be caught. So the couple called me again. This time, I talked to the cat and explained how much he was loved, then gave him instructions for getting home. I told him how to be careful while traveling and encouraged him to find his own way back to his family. Some time after I spoke with him, he came through the cat door of his home.

Another successful case was that of Vicki Brink, who called me about her lost cat, Missy. When I communicated with Missy, she complained that she was locked in a greenhouse and couldn't get out. She showed me her route and indicated the distance she had traveled. Vicki found Missy in the exact location I had described, locked in a garage that had been used as a greenhouse by the former residents.

The precision of details in these cases can be astonishing. For example, when Pam and Geoff Oakley-Whiting called about Tazz, their red Maine coon cat, I told them that I believed Tazz was hiding in some old farmhouse buildings, and I gave them the direction and distance I felt he had traveled. But they said that there were no old buildings in their area, only new houses. I had distinctly seen turn-of-the-century construction with old stone work and dark wood. I decided that I must have been wrong, but encouraged them to explore further. They called me back to say that they had found an old compound, just as I had described, and that it had been the site of a nudist colony around 1900. When they went there to look for Tazz, they found rock buildings and high windows just as I had described, but no Tazz. There was a large dog running loose on the property. The couple asked that the dog be locked up while the search proceeded. That evening, Tazz showed up on his own doorstep. We don't know for sure, but we think he finally came out of hiding and ran home once the dog was no longer a threat.

Sometimes when I am right about a lost animal, there is no joy in it. When a woman called about her errant cat, I was fairly sure that a coyote had eaten him. In fact, I even saw the coyote, sensed that it was female with a litter to feed, and got precise information about where the woman might find coyote scat containing the cat's fur for confirmation. The woman verified my information about a coyote being in the area and found evidence of her cat's fur in coyote scat in the location I had indicated.

Why It's Difficult

Apart from all the factors that make intuitive communication challenging in the first place, there are some special conditions that apply to lost-animal work. Usually people are very upset when they call. The situation may be critical; they want immediate attention and the pressure is on the communicator to perform. The first thing people ask is whether their animal is alive or dead. But what if, as the communicator, your information is wrong? It can happen, especially in cases in which the animal died suddenly. I worked on a lost dog case in which I saw the dog running free through the hills. In fact, I later learned that the dog had been killed instantly upon his escape; a tree branch had fallen on his head. My assessment of this error was that the dog did not actually realize he was dead. He had escaped through the fence to go off on an adventure, and because death was so swift he continued on his adventure, unaware that he was in spirit form.

I have observed that time can get distorted when working with lost animals. I worked on the case of a dog who had been hit by a car and was on the run. I would get locations for her — a brown house with a wishing well in the garden, the grain room at a large stable — and then hear from the search party that the location was accurate and the dog had been seen there, but that now she was gone. The dog was staying one step ahead of me. Finally, she wandered into the yard of a kind, animal-savvy person who wooed her inside and then called her people.

I ask my clients not to tell me what they think happened or to tell me the findings of other animal communicators. It is hard to be objective if I have too much subjective input from other sources.

Sometimes a lost animal can be extremely reticent and hard to contact. The animal may be fearful or in pain. I've contacted animals who tell me that they are dead, and then refuse to talk about how they died. They simply do not want their people to know the unpleasant details. I have also talked to a few animals who just didn't want to come home, although this is rare. It happened with Jody Erwin's cat, Piaget, who escaped into an area unfamiliar to him when Jody took him with her to visit her daughter.

I told Jody to search behind her daughter's neighborhood for a gray house with white gravel in the back garden, owned by an older couple. Jody found the house, and the couple who lived there had seen Piaget in their yard the day before. So then I had to find out his new location. At one point, Jody and I were talking by cell phone, and I was helping her chase Piaget all around the neighborhood. I told her to find a wooden house with pampas grass in the yard. She found it, saw Piaget, approached him — and he darted away. We found him over and over, but we couldn't catch up with him. The chase took about a month. Finally, sated with adventure, he showed up looking for some dinner at the back door of the house he'd escaped from.

One final factor that makes this process difficult is that you may not get instant results. Animals are on animal time, not people time — especially cats. Cats take forever to do everything. I've had people e-mail me six months or even a year after I worked on their case to tell me that their cat was, in fact, alive as I had thought and had just shown up at the house looking fine and carrying on as if nothing unusual had happened.

HOW TO FIND LOST ANIMALS

The best advice I can give for finding lost animals is the same advice I give for doing any other intuitive communication: Follow what you are getting; go with what is coming in.

Naturally, you will want the animal to be alive, but always follow what you are getting. Based on evidence in the case, you might be tempted to make certain logical conclusions. Resist doing that; instead, follow what you are getting.

You will first need to get the details of the case. If you don't know the animal, ask for a complete description or a photograph. Have the person tell you exactly what happened. Ask for the facts, nothing else. Ask whether there are any verified sightings of the animal.

Many communicators also ask to be provided with a map of the area where the animal was lost. You may work from a map if you like, using a pendulum or dowsing rod to help you determine where on the map to best search for the animal.[1] I find that I do not need to have a map in front of me. I simply use my intuition to view the terrain remotely and interview the animal to determine where she traveled. After I finish getting all the details of a case, I will often consult a general map of the area using an Internet map site. If any of my data match the details on the map, I can direct people to a specific river, park, or street that corresponds to what I saw intuitively.

Alive or Dead?

Determining whether the animal is alive or dead is the pivotal step. Whatever you decide at this point informs everything else you do with a lost animal. The way I determine whether the animal is dead or alive is to ask her point blank and explain how important it is that she convey clear, accurate information. Then I turn my attention to my intuition and record whatever comes in. I also check internally to see how I feel about the information I am getting. Does it feel like the animal is alive or dead? If the answer I get is not clear, I ask again until I get an answer that feels more solid. I ask to get the answer in words, as that is my most reliable mode of intuitive communication. When working with lost animals, you should work in your own best mode of reception.

What's the Big Picture?

Once I feel fairly secure about an animal's condition (though I am never certain), I ask her to tell me generally what happened. If I feel that she's dead, I might ask how she died. Then I would get words or maybe a picture of how she died. If I feel that she's alive, I may ask something like, "Where are you and what's happening?" In response, I might get a feeling of her being trapped, or she might send me a statement like, "I'm lost and I don't know how to get home." Or she might show me a picture of a house and indicate that she is with someone.

Once in a while, I get a smart-aleck animal who says she is just out having a great time. In those cases, I admonish the animal to stop torturing her person and get herself home. I had two cases like that, involving the cats of two women who are friends but who live on different continents. Ellen Spiegel, who lives in California, told her friend Sylvie Maier in the Netherlands to e-mail me when Sylvie lost her cat, Beertje. When I contacted Beertje, he showed me that he was off having an amorous affair. I urged him to go home, and he did so by the next day. Then, a year later when I was teaching in the Netherlands at Sylvie's invitation, I got a call from Ellen in California. Ellen's male cat Pepper (aka Pepperoni) had been missing for two days and she was frantic. I contacted Pepper while Ellen waited on the line. Pepper told me that he was off on a lark, but not too far from home. I told him that he had to get home immediately because Ellen was really upset. She called me back a few minutes later to say that Pepper appeared at the door as soon as we got off the phone.

What Happened in Detail?

Once I have the big picture and feel fairly comfortable that I am on the right track, I ask the animal to show me what happened from the moment she left until the present. As I get this information, it is as if I am inside the animal, looking out of her eyes and retracing all of her movements. Sometimes, though, I will be looking down on a scene as if with a bird's-eye view. To determine which direction the animal went, I orient myself to the front door of the building from which the animal escaped. Then, when I talk to the people, I am able to tell them her exact route. Usually I can see the twists and turns the animal took and get some estimate of how far she went. I was actually told in one case that bloodhounds, called in to work on a case after my report, followed exactly the route I described.

When I interview a lost animal, I ask her to show me what she saw along the route and I jot down any landmarks that could provide clues to her whereabouts. If I feel that the animal has been stolen, I then try to get the details of that scenario, including a description of the people involved and their car, and any clues to the motivation for the theft.

Where Are You Now?

I try to use my intuition to track the animal's movements all the way to her current location. Then I ask a series of questions designed to get as many clues as possible about where she is at the moment when we are speaking. I ask things like, "Do you know the way home? Can you get home? Are you with people? If so, can you describe them? Where are you right now, as I am speaking with you? What do you smell, taste, see, hear, and feel where you are right now? Are you injured or hurt in any way? Are you hungry or thirsty? How are you feeling? Do you want to go home?" Depending on the answers, I will advise and comfort the animal as best I can.

Get Outside Help

If there are other animals in the household, I get their names and descriptions and then ask them to tell me anything they know about what is going on with the lost animal. They may have seen something or they may have information derived from intuitive contact with the lost animal. I also ask universal knowledge whether there is any additional information I may have missed.

When Is It Time to Give Up?

I will work on a case twice or sometimes three times, and then if I discover nothing useful I give up. I advise my clients to do everything they can to find their animal within the limits of their time and resources, and then if nothing turns up they may have to stop searching so intensely. It is good to keep reposting flyers and checking the shelters and clinics for a while, but the process of searching can eventually get out of hand. Sometimes, if the search has led nowhere, people may have to face the fact that they will never know what happened or see their animal again.

EXERCISES: FINDING LOST ANIMALS

If you have a friend or an acquaintance who has lost an animal, offer to help but be sure to explain that you are a beginner. Get a picture or description of the lost animal and any other animals in the household. Get a map of the area where the animal was lost. If the lost animal is your own, you can still try all the exercises, but you may find it more difficult to be objective. You may also want to get outside help by calling a professional communicator to work on the case.

When working on a lost-animal case, I would recommend that you do the long version of the focusing and connecting steps that are summarized in chapter 8 (pages 129–130). Once you have gone through the steps and connected with the lost animal, you are ready to start the following exercises. When you are through, report your results to the animal's person.

Exercise 1: Alive or Dead? Getting the Big Picture

Ask the animal if she is alive or dead. Go with any feelings that come in about this. Ask the animal to be really clear. Stress the importance of her answer and the need for accuracy. Ask her to tell you in words, pictures, or whatever is your best mode of reception. Once you feel that you have received an answer, ask her what is happening. If you feel that she is dead, ask her how it happened. If you feel that she is alive, ask her where she is and why she has not come home. Get the big picture.

Exercise 2: What Happened?

Now ask the lost animal to show you where she went from the moment she left to the present. See or feel those past scenes as if you were inside the animal, going through them again. Try to get details, landmarks, and anything that will help the searchers find the animal. Continue asking what happened until you reach her current location.

Exercise 3: Where Are You Now?

Find out as much as you can about where the animal is at the moment you are speaking. Here are some possible questions to ask:

- Do you know the way home? Can you get home?
- Are you with people? If so, can you describe them?
- Where are you right now, as I am speaking with you?
- What do you smell, taste, see, hear, and feel where you are right now?
- Are you injured or hurt in any way?
- Are you hungry or thirsty?
- How are you emotionally?
- Do you want to go home?

Give advice and comfort to the animal as best you can. Explain what you are doing and tell her that you will tell her people all the information she has given you.

Exercise 4: Ask the Other Animals

Ask the other animals in the household if they saw anything or know anything about what happened. Ask if they have been in intuitive contact with the animal and, if so, what they have learned.

Exercise 5: Ask Universal Knowledge

Ask universal knowledge whether there is anything else you need to know about this case or if there is anything you missed.

Part Five

Communicating
with Nature

Chapter Fourteen

The World's Wildlife

We have lost the intimate relationship with wildlife that our ancestors had. Some people even think that we can live without wildlife, but that's an illusion perpetrated by the forces now destroying the earth. Global corporations and superpower governments are now so greedy for power and profit that they are ravaging the earth's ecosystems. No lie is too big for them if it serves to perpetuate and protect this unfettered onslaught.

In truth, we can no more live without wildlife than we can live without air. We need insects to pollinate, bats to eat insects, birds to spread seed, and coyotes to control rodents. While we depend upon wildlife for the things we need to survive, wild creatures do not similarly depend upon us — except that they need us to stop destroying their homes and killing them off, species by species.

Our indigenous ancestors related with wildlife differently than we do. Animals were considered to be sacred spiritual beings, thanked for their services to humans and consulted as oracles of truth and foretellers of the future. Animals who were killed for food were ritually honored and thanked. Contrast this with our current factory farming system. Domestication of animals sprang from cooperative and reciprocal relationships between our ancient ancestors and wild animals. When we modern humans learn again to communicate in the ancient way with wild animals, these alliances are revived and we begin a journey that leads toward reverence for all life.

When you talk with a wild animal, you will use all the same techniques you learned for talking with cats, dogs, and horses. Most wild animals will be interested in talking, but because they aren't enmeshed in our lives the experience may feel more like a discourse between disparate nations. The way most wild animals relate to the world is so different from our lifestyles that they are almost incomprehensible to us — a strange and separate culture.

We've been emotionally separated from wildlife for a long time because alienation from nature is integral to most modern cultures. It would be nice, when we first start talking with wild animals again, for us to tell them how much we appreciate them and why they are important to us. Wildlife have not heard this from most humans for many, many centuries.

When you connect with a wild animal, you won't be able to call him by name unless he tells you his name. And you will have a harder time verifying the messages you receive. One option is to ask questions about the biology of the animal and then check your answers in a field guide. You may also find verification in the actions and events that occur following your conversation.

This happened to me once during a class I was teaching. The class was held in a building with high windows that opened onto the roof. The design of the roof was such that a peacock from a children's farm next door was able to stand on the roof and peer down at our class through the windows.[1] Not only was he peering at us, he was calling. If you have ever heard a peacock call, you will understand why the entire class came to a stop at this point. Since he wasn't prepared to cease, we decided to talk with him and find out what he wanted.

He had several messages for us. He wanted our attention, and requested that we come over to the farm and visit him. But his strongest message was that one of the animals at the farm was in trouble and he wanted us to do something about it. So the entire class got up and headed for the farm. On our way there, a woman riding a bicycle came toward us shouting, "Quick, do something! There is a baby goat in the moat!" One of the newborn goats at the farm had fallen into the moat that surrounded the farm. We managed to save the baby goat because of the peacock's warning, and he got his wish: We all came over to see him.

WILDLIFE IN YOUR BACKYARD

The best place to start looking for wildlife to talk with is in your own home and yard. If you search, you will find wild animals everywhere, no matter where you live. It doesn't have to be a lion, a dolphin, or some other impressive animal; insects, birds, and reptiles are wildlife, too. J. Allen Boone[2] devoted a fourth of his book to his incredible relationship with a fly named Freddie. Any wild animal may be the doorway into the natural world. Pick a wild animal that you see in, around, or traveling past your home. Establish a relationship with this animal through regular conversations. Refer to a good field guide to assess what kinds of verifiable questions you might ask. If you chose a bird to work with, you might ask the bird if it is male or female, how many eggs it usually has, and what size and color those eggs are. Ask if the bird migrates or stays in your area over the winter. Then check your answers in a field guide.

You can invite wild animals to visit you by making your home a haven for them.

Here are some ways to attract wildlife to your backyard:[3]

- Plant flowers that are attractive to birds and butterflies in your yard or in containers on a patio or windowsill.
- Install nesting boxes for birds and bats.
- Place a birdbath in a safe, open place in your yard.
- Put up wildlife-friendly fencing, with gaps or other features that allow wildlife to more easily move through their territories (and pass through your yard).
- Use safe, nontoxic alternatives to poisons for pest and weed control in your yard; otherwise, you could end up poisoning wildlife higher up the food chain. A good organic nursery should be able to supply these alternative products. (Encourage your neighbors to do the same.)
- Support local organic farmers who don't use toxins; buy their organic vegetables.
- Install cat fencing (see the resources section at the back of this book) in part of your yard to contain your cats and prevent them from killing birds and other animals.

Once you have enhanced your backyard, send out an intuitive message to the wildlife explaining what you have done and inviting the animals to come visit.

When you communicate intuitively with wildlife, you will say, think, or feel the words you wish to convey, assuming, as usual, that your message is getting across. Try interviewing the wildlife in your yard about their daily lives, playing the role of a reporter and following any interesting stories that arise. You might even ask for advice or guidance from the wildlife you encounter. You may discover, as did Marianne and Willem Pikkaart who sent me this story, that the feelings these animals have for you are deeper than you suspect. They write:

One day a blackbird flew against my garden window and fell to the ground. Suddenly a cat appeared and started approaching the bird. I knocked loudly on the window to scare the cat, and my husband went out and drove the cat away. We saw that the bird was still alive. I recognized that this bird had little ones nearby and that we must try to save her. So, carefully, we took the blackbird to our green-house and closed the door so that the cat couldn't get in.

After a few hours, we saw that the blackbird was moving. A little later she was looking fine, so we decided to set her free. She flew out of the greenhouse to a fence, looked at us for a while, and then went to her nest. Case closed, we thought. But what happened next was really unbeliev-able. My husband was doing some gardening and I was in the house, and we both heard it: A choir of at least a hun-dred different birds started to sing all at once. We have never heard anything like it before or since. Perhaps, just perhaps, they were thanking us for saving the blackbird.

WILDLIFE PESTS

"But what," you may ask, "if all I have at my house are wildlife pests?" Well, first of all, one person's pest is another person's darling.

One of my favorite animals is the skunk, smell and all, and I'm sure some entomologist somewhere loves mosquitoes. If all you have are pesty wild animals at your house, then my advice would be to talk with *them*. One of the most intriguing conversations I ever had was with a yellow jacket. I asked him about his friends, activities, favorite foods, and feelings for humans. It was magical to listen to a yellow jacket discussing his friends. As for humans, he described us as unreasonable and completely prejudiced toward his kind. I had to agree. That conversation changed my interactions with yellow jackets. With my newfound camaraderie for an insect that I used to fear, I now politely ask yellow jackets to move away or go outside when they are bothering me, and I usually get a positive response.

In her book, *The Voice of the Infinite in the Small*,[4] Joanne Lauck encourages us to completely revise our relationships with the animals we consider to be pests. I agree; we must do that. I have not yet achieved Lauck's level of comfort with all species, but I have changed my feelings for many animals I used to fear and loathe. I did so by talking with them and finding out who they really are. Talking with an insect or some other animal that you dislike or fear can be most illuminating. Try talking with the fly that's buzzing around your kitchen. For inspiration, read about Boone's relationship with Freddie.

Dealing with pests was actually Boone's forte. He talked to the ants in his kitchen, politely, as equals, and successfully got them to leave. He talked to the gophers in his friend's pasture and got them to relocate. His technique was simply to be respectful, treat other beings as equals, and make reasonable requests. I would add a fourth tactic: offer recompense. If you want the ants to leave your house, offer them some food or sugar somewhere outside. It is certainly worth a try before you jump to poisons and mayhem.

Petra and Freek Gout have been very successful at this. Each year, they vacation in the south of France. When they get to their cottage, Freek always starts the vacation by chatting with the ants. He greets them and asks them to please stay out of the cottage while he is visiting. They've never had any ant problems, except for one year when their journey had been rushed and they arrived at the cottage exhausted. As a consequence, Freek neglected to have his chat with the ants. Within a day, the cottage was deluged with ants. Freek immediately went to speak with them, and soon the ants were gone again.

I do need to insert a caveat: Although I do my best to coexist peacefully with the wildlife who live with and around me, sometimes it just doesn't work. My experience with a nest of thousands of yellow jackets in my front yard was not so convivial. I tried not to disturb them and I was willing to share my yard, but when they got to a certain critical mass they just started attacking when we walked by the nest, which wasn't safe. In that situation, I had to destroy the nest. The poisonous spiders around my house now generally stay out of the house at my urging, but they haven't seemed to jolly up to my idea that they breed less. So I do some baby-spider population control and relocate some of the adults. I think that when wildlife are entrenched and consider your home their home, it can be hard to shift things. Some kind of control may be the only solution. But if you search, you may be able to find a method that is nontoxic and nonviolent.[5]

ENCOUNTERS IN THE WILD

When you are out walking or hiking, you will probably see many wild animals. They may not stay around you for long, as most wild animals now wisely seek to avoid humans. You can counter that tendency by mentally greeting them, explaining that you are learning to speak their language, and then asking them a question. Even if they bolt or fly off, you can continue the conversation. In intuitive communication, the animal does not have to be present. Often, wild animals will react positively to your intuitive overture and stop to talk. You may even find yourself in a two-way interaction.

My veterinarian, Lisa Pesch, told me this experience over lunch one day. She was hiking in a high meadow in Yosemite and she sat down on a large rock to rest. Almost at once, a Belding's ground squirrel appeared in front of her. She was so happy to see the squirrel that she started to sing to it. More squirrels came, then more, until she had a meadow full of squirrels listening to her sing. It was so incredible that she couldn't even think of stopping. She kept singing until it got dark, when she finally forced herself to say good-bye and leave them.

Of course, you should not approach a bear, mountain lion, or other potentially dangerous animal in the wild unless you know what you are doing. There are other, safer ways to encounter wildlife. However, some of these are not so straightforward. You can go to zoos to meet wildlife, but I find zoos so depressing as to be almost unbearable. If I go to a zoo, it is for the express purpose of trying to cheer up the animals in whatever way I can. Traveling to exotic places to interact with wild animals — dolphin swims and the like — can certainly be thrilling. But such trips can also be exploitive of both the animals and the local human populations. If you seek out trips organized by naturalists who are concerned and sensitive about these issues and who work with the locals in an equitable way, you will be addressing some of these issues, but not the underlying inequity of humans yet again taking from wildlife — in this case the experience of being in their home — without giving anything back.

I think one of the best ways to meet wildlife is to volunteer at a wildlife rehabilitation center. There you can safely forge a friendship over time with the animals in your care, and you will be giving them something back. Although not all the animals you care for will survive, you will have the joy of setting at least some of them free again. The relationships you have with these animals will stay with you forever. Armie Scarlett told me this story about a bird she befriended at a wildlife clinic:

> I cared for an evening grosbeak who had been attacked by a cat and lost all his tail feathers. He was quite fierce-looking and had a loud whistle. Whenever I had to feed him and clean the cage, he would try to escape; I dreaded doing that job. One day, I decided not to be intimidated any longer and I opened the door and let him out into the clinic room. He flew up to the top of the cupboard, and when it was time to go back in his cage he allowed me to catch him. This bird was with us for at least a year, waiting for his tail feathers to grow. We would talk to him and look at his tail and praise him for any tiny new feathers.
>
> Winter came, and the grosbeak was the only patient left at the clinic. So another volunteer offered to take him home with her to allow the center to close for the season. A month later, the volunteer called to tell me that the grosbeak had escaped into the woods near her house, which is about a mile from my house. It was very cold. She put out heat lamps and heating pads and food, hoping that he would come back, but nothing happened. Two days later, after two freezing nights, I saw a grosbeak sitting on the edge of my roof. I said, "Hey, are you a grosbeak?" He whistled. I said, "Are you our grosbeak?"

He turned around and showed me his tail, minus tail feathers!

Alas, once he was back in his cage amid much celebration and wonderment, the grosbeak went into a decline and died. The cold nights and the trip through the woods had been too much for him. But how did he find his way to my house? Did he mean to? Was it just chance? We'll never know.

ANIMALS AS GUIDES AND ORACLES

Wild animals can serve as our guides and helpers if they choose to. Throughout history, there have been stories of dolphins saving shipwrecked people. You may find a wild animal guide yourself once you start talking with wildlife. In her book *Lady of the Beasts,*[6] Buffie Johnson catalogs hundreds of prehistoric artifacts that demonstrate an enduring human fascination with and reverence for wild animals. Some of the artifacts and cave drawings date back almost one hundred thousand years to the Pleistocene Age. Only within the last few thousand years have humans become alienated from wildlife and nature. For most of the human experience, we related to wildlife as our kin, asked them for advice, and considered them to be sacred sources of truth and knowledge. We can do this again if we want to.

In her well-researched book about omens, oracles, and divination, *When Oracles Speak,*[7] Dianne Skafte brings the premodern world back to life and allows us to imagine a time when people saw the world as "ensouled," believing that everything was truly alive, brimming with consciousness, and gazing back at us. She shows us a world vastly different from the one we inhabit — a world in which people looked to nature for guidance and messages.

Bees, widely revered as messengers and oracles, were worshipped as gods and goddesses in some cultures. Crow calls were thought to be of great significance; entire books were written on the subject of their interpretation.

We modern humans can choose once again to be open to the power of wildlife and invite wild animals into our lives. This story, told to me by my client Valerie Parks, shows how strong their presence can be:

> Large cats have been a major feature in my life. I have had wild bobcats even move into my house. For some reason, they are my guides.
>
> I used to live in the mountains, and it was my routine to go into town once a week to visit my grandmother and stock up on groceries. On my way home from one of these trips, at about midnight, I went around a curve on the canyon road just in time to see a mountain lion leap onto the road from the rocks above. She stopped right in the middle of the road, making it impossible to get by. Since I was mesmerized by her power and beauty anyway, I didn't want to move. That was about twenty-seven years ago, before I knew anything about animal guides and all the rest, so I didn't realize that this was more important than it seemed. The lioness kept me there, just staring at me and not moving a muscle. After about twenty minutes, she just got up, walked to the other side of the road, and sat down as if to say, "OK, you may go now."
>
> I drove on, and when I got home I found the police at my house. It turned out that my ex-husband (a violent alcoholic) had broken into my house and chased my dogs away, and was waiting for me to come home. He had a jar

of battery acid and was planning to "fix me." The police had only been there for about ten minutes when I arrived. They were called by a neighbor who had seen my dogs and knew there must be something wrong at my house. If the lioness hadn't stopped me, I would have stumbled into this scene before the police got there. Whenever I get depressed in life, I think to myself, "That lioness saved me for a reason, and I feel guided and encouraged."

When we can once again relate to wildlife and all of life on earth as our guides, our teachers, and our equals, we can begin to explore the wisdom and assistance they have to offer us. They offer us these gifts freely, without expectation, but in exchange can we do any less than work to ensure their health and happiness?

EXERCISES: WILDLIFE

When you contact a wild animal, you will follow the same techniques for focusing and connecting that you have already learned. You can use the long or short version of these methods and work with your eyes open or closed. These techniques are summarized in chapter 8, on pages 129–130. If you decide to do some interviews, you may want to pick questions from the list at the end of chapter 9.

Since you will not know the animal's name, ask the animal what he or she would like to be called. You would do the same for any new person you might meet. If the animal offers no name, simply use the generic name for the animal, such as hedgehog, or firefly, or fence lizard. You may find that every wild animal you approach flees from you. Do not despair. It probably isn't something about you; it's just the way the animals have come to relate to us these days. You can still have the conversation. As I am writing this, I hear a hawk calling as it flies over my house. I can sit in my office and have a conversation with that hawk, who has now flown away, just as well as if I were outside and the hawk were right above me in a tree. You can have a conversation with any wild animal you see fleetingly, or even a wild animal that you remember from the past. All you need to do is connect with the animal from your heart and start talking.

There are a lot of exercises in this section. Read through them and choose the ones that appeal to you. Use your notebook to record the results of your conversations and any other observations.

Interacting with the Wildlife around You

Exercise 1: Wildlife in Your Backyard

Assess the population of wild animals that live in and around your home. Remember, insects are wild animals, too. Once you have determined which animals you might work with, select an animal you feel attracted to and comfortable with. Initiate a conversation with the animal. Introduce yourself, and explain what you are doing and that you are a student. Ask for the animal's assistance. Ask if he has a name he wants you to use (at which point you may find out that he is a she). Tell him why you appreciate him and what he means to you personally. Explain that you would like to continue having conversations with him and find out if he is agreeable. Follow up in future conversations by: 1) asking verifiable questions about his biology (and checking your answers in a field guide), and 2) interviewing him using some of the questions from the list in chapter 9 or some that you make up on your own.

Exercise 2: Attracting Wildlife to You

If you love butterflies, you can probably attract more of them to your home just by going outside and announcing that you would like that to happen. You might also do something physically to your home to attract more of the kinds of wild animals you like — for example, installing plants that wildlife like, a birdbath, or a dragonfly pond. For more ideas, ask a local nursery or ecology center, or research the topic at the library or on the Internet. Once you have completed your enhancements, tell the animals what you've done and invite them to come visit.

Exercise 3: Asking for Advice

Pick a wild animal that you feel emotionally connected with for this exercise. This could be an animal you met in the past or an animal you know now. To connect, simply close your eyes and imagine seeing an image of the animal. Ask the animal's name. Ask if the animal has any advice for you. You may leave the question open-ended, or you may specify a topic — from the frivolous to the very serious — about which you would like advice. Keep asking questions until you understand the advice the animal is giving you. Thank the animal.

Exercise 4: Talking with an Animal You Dislike or Fear

Don't worry; to do this exercise you don't have to get close to or even imagine being near this animal. Select an animal that you dislike or fear. Choose several questions from the list at the end of chapter 9 to ask of this animal. Think of the last time you saw this animal (even if only in a picture). Close your eyes and imagine the animal, but keep it at a safe and comfortable distance from you. Introduce yourself, explain what you are doing, and ask the animal's name. Ask the questions you have selected. When you are finished, ask if the animal has anything to add. Tell the animal anything you wish to express. Thank the animal and end the interview.

Encounters in the Wild

Exercise 5: Meeting Animals on a Hike

Offer a mental greeting to the wildlife you meet when you are on a hike. Extend your appreciation and any positive observations you wish to make about the animals. Explain that you are learning to speak their language and ask if they would like to talk. (Do not approach any wildlife that could hurt you.) You might try singing to them. Ask the animals anything you are curious about, even if they turn and run from you. Remember, you don't have to be right next to an animal to converse intuitively. If you are speaking with an animal you see regularly on your walks, ask for the animal's name. If you get a name, the next time you go hiking greet the animal by the name he gave you.

Exercise 6: Working at a Wildlife Clinic

If you sign up to work at a wildlife clinic, you will probably find certain individuals and even certain species of wildlife that appeal to you more than others. Work intuitively with the animals for whom you feel this affinity. You can interview the animals and do some of the medical intuition and energy healing exercises that are described in chapter 12.

Exercise 7: Finding a Wild Animal Guide

You may already know a wild animal who has come forward to be your guide. Even if you're not already aware of having a guide, through paying more attention to wildlife you may find one particular individual who is always right there for you. Ask to know who your guide is, and the knowledge will come to you. Once you identify this guide, extend your gratitude. Thank this individual for offering assistance. Then ask to receive guidance; in time, it will come to you. Ask your guide for answers to questions you have about your life or about something in the future. If you liked doing the journey described at the end of chapter 8, try it again with your wild animal guide.

Chapter Fifteen

Plants and
the Landscape

You may have been on board until now. "Animals? Well, they look like us and act like us — at least some of them do — so, yes, it makes sense that we could possibly talk with them. But plants? Mountains?" I think it's easier to make this leap of logic if you spend a lot of time around plants and out in nature. Every devoted gardener I've met, when pressed, admits to talking to plants and receiving responses. They describe getting a feeling about what would be good for the plant or what the plant needs, and they readily identify this as feedback from the plant.

Modern humans relate to plants and the landscape as objects. But, as I mentioned in the Introduction, indigenous people living in the way of their ancestors relate to plants, trees, rocks, rivers, mountains, and all of nature as having spirit and consciousness. They treat nonhumans as if they were people, and most traditions are careful to address the spirit of each being — especially those they must kill for survival. This worldview has largely been lost to us. However, it is still accessible, and I believe it to be the expression of our true nature.

When I was doing research for this book, I came across the story of George Washington Carver in a book called *The Secret Life of Plants*.[1] For me, Carver exemplifies the ancient spirit that lies below the surface in all of us. How had I missed this incredible story throughout my education? I am sure most of you haven't heard it, either. Carver may be known as a genius and credited with developing uses for the peanut and the sweet potato, but I doubt that botany classes delve into this man's life. To me, his character and his relationship with plants are more fascinating than those accomplishments.

Carver was born into slavery in Missouri just before the Civil War. Described as a frail child who possessed an unusual, high-pitched voice, he was a loner. He wandered the foothills of the Ozark Mountains searching out plants. As a young child, he scrounged materials from the countryside and built a greenhouse by himself. He used plants from the wild as medicines to effect miraculous cures on people's domestic animals. When asked what he did all day alone, he replied that he went to his hospital to take care of his sick plants. People began bringing him their sick houseplants. He sang to the plants, gave them special soil, and took them to play in the sun during the day. When asked how he accomplished his cures, he said that the flowers and everything in the woods talked to him. He just listened to them and loved them.

Carver went on to receive a master's degree in agricultural chemistry, and eventually headed the agricultural department of the Normal and Industrial Institute in Tuskegee, Alabama. His accomplishments were outstanding. He revolutionized Southern agriculture by discovering the utility of peanuts and sweet potatoes in all forms of industry. With the help of the plants, he developed hundreds of dyes from natural sources when dyes were in short supply during World War I. Yet his methods remained frustratingly obscure to those around him. He claimed that his techniques came to him as flashes of inspiration when he walked in the woods. When pressed, he replied that the secrets he found were in the plants and that all anyone had to do to discover them was to love the plants enough.

Here's another little-known fact: Luther Burbank, known as "The Wizard of Horticulture," produced the equivalent of one entirely new plant specimen every week during his working career — an unmatched accomplishment. He, too, professed to talk to his plants and send them love, and was reportedly convinced that plants could understand him when he spoke to them.[2]

WHAT'S WRONG WITH THIS PICTURE?

How can this be? How can these acknowledged geniuses believe that plants can talk and that we can hear them, while we know nothing of this and were taught that such ideas are lunatic? How can native people all over the world have a rich, productive relationship with nature while we are cut off and clueless? The answer, according to some of our greatest thinkers on this topic, is the flawed cosmology of modern human society. It does not reflect reality; it is insupportable. We believe — no, we are taught to believe — that all matter lacks consciousness, emotion, and spirit. Only humans get to have those things. That's the old cosmology.

The new cosmology, articulated by Targ,[3] de Quincey,[4] and others,[5,6] says that all of nature is in communication with all of its constituents. All matter — down to the single cell, the atom, and the quantum particle — has consciousness and emotions. All matter and all energy in the universe is sentient. In other words, all matter can feel. This new cosmology asks the question: How could we possibly have evolved from a dead, nonsentient, nonfeeling matrix of matter? Answer: We couldn't have, and we didn't. Nature is alive — though she's not doing too well these days — and you can talk with her.

MAKING YOUR GARDEN GROW

In *The Secret Life of Plants*, the authors recount a host of experiments conducted on plants to monitor physiological changes in response to various stimuli. In experiments conducted in the United States, Europe, and Russia, researchers found the same results: Plants can sense our feelings, react to positive and negative stimuli, read our minds, and anticipate our actions.[7] The evidence in these experiments is very convincing, but it has been ignored by most scientists. Why is that? I'd say it's because modern science is based on the old cosmology. Most scientists are invested in the worldview that all life forms other than humans are nonfeeling blobs of protoplasm. To believe otherwise is to challenge the whole premise of science as we know it. It is time for just such a challenge.

While scientists may choose to ignore these incredible discoveries, you don't have to. I believe that plants can communicate intuitively just as animals can, and that you can receive information intuitively from plants. You will do this in the same way, using the same techniques that you've used with animals. Your interactions with plants can be just as intuitive and emotional as those you have with animals.

Start with your garden and the plants in and around your

home. If you don't have a yard, you can talk with your houseplants or the potted plants on your balcony. Tell them how much you appreciate them, and encourage them to grow and be healthy. Interview the plants and ask about their biology, then check your answers. Send love to the plants like Carver and Burbank did. Ask the plants about their secrets and maybe, if you love them enough, they will tell you.

A student named Laura Lathrop received a communication from a tree during one of my classes, which she was later able to verify. She was communicating with a Monterey pine tree. She asked the tree how it was doing. The tree told her that it needed more water and complained that one of its branches, about one-third of the way up the tree's trunk, was somehow wrong or sick. A tree surgeon was subsequently called in to examine the tree, but not told anything about the communication. He found that the pine tree had an infestation of beetles in a limb that was about one-third of the way up the trunk. He also advised that the tree be given more water because, he explained, pine trees become susceptible to beetle attack when they don't get enough water.

If you have an insect infestation on one of your plants, try talking with the insects. Ask why they are eating the plant. Ask if the insects will agree to eat a little less. Then talk with the plant and ask why it is being attacked. Maybe there is something you need to do to make the plant stronger. Then again, maybe you will learn that the insects and the plants need to do this and that you just need to stay out of it.

If you have weeds or other plants that you don't want in your garden, talk with them. Ask them what they are up to. See if there is some bargain you can strike with them in order for you to coexist. Offer them your appreciation and send them love, too.

The people who created the Findhorn experimental garden in

Scotland grew plants on a sandy wasteland where no one thought it possible. The secret to their success, they said, was an alliance with nature spirits — those spirits thought to inhabit the plants and the land.[8] Celtic folklore is replete with references to the spirits found in nature — in fact, so are most folk traditions. You, too, can work with the spirits of nature. Call on them, acknowledge them, and ask for their assistance. It is not too late for us to recover the wisdom and the ways of our ancestors.

THE WILD EARTH

For millennia, humans have turned to plants for healing. The Cherokee tradition holds that plants took pity on humans and offered us the remedies for all our ailments. Native people and all the master herbalists I have ever encountered, approach medicinal plants in the same way: respectfully, as if the plants were human. They consider the *plant's* needs as well as their own. They tell the plants what kind of healing is needed and ask for the plant's help. They leave offerings of thanks: cornmeal, tobacco, and sweets. This is how people originally discovered the individual healing properties of plants. This is the way all our plant medicines came into use: through a respectful, equal interchange.[9] Steven Buhner, in his book *The Lost Language of Plants*,[10] notes that few people realize this fact — or the fact that many of the medicines in use today were derived in some manner from ancient plant medicines.

Flower essences are another form of plant healing that came from the intuitive interaction of humans and plants.[11] People communicated intuitively with flowers and asked them what emotional conditions they could address and heal. For example, lavender was found to be calming. Once the quality was determined, the flower essence was prepared by placing flower blossoms in water for a period of time. Then the flowers were removed, and the remaining water was said to have taken on the essence of the flower. When administered to an animal, person, or another plant, this essence conveys the emotional component associated with the individual flower.

Plants offer us their help, but that is not their purpose for being here. They have their own reality and they have community, just as we do. They relate to each other and rely upon each other. They form societies. Humans are usually oblivious to this. I once heard Julia Butterfly Hill speak about the time she spent sitting in Luna, an ancient redwood tree in Northern California.[12] Julia climbed into Luna's branches to protect the tree from being cut down. While she and Luna watched, the rest of the old-growth trees in the surrounding forest were clear-cut. The operation was terrifying; helicopters swerved around Luna, air-lifting out the bodies of her kin. Once the carnage was complete and Julia and Luna stood alone in a clear-cut, Julia said that Luna began to weep. Sap in the form of tears appeared all over her trunk. Her roots — her connection to all of her friends, to her community — were severed. Julia said that she felt profound grief from Luna. Who better than Julia to bring us the message that trees have feelings?

When I teach a class in communicating with nature, it seems that every student remembers a tree from childhood — a tree that was a confidante and a good friend, a tree that was strong and beautiful. How did we get so far away from the truth we knew about nature when we were young? Trees are our teachers. They are incredibly wise. Some are more ancient than history. They can be our guides. People used to consult trees as oracles of truth. You can again have trees for your friends. Just talk with them, sit with your back against them, and touch them.

THE SPIRIT OF PLACE

Just as I believe that you can talk with plants, I also believe that you can talk with the various features of the landscape — waterfalls, mountains, rivers, and caves. I also believe that each place on earth has a spirit — a soul, if you will — and that you can connect intuitively with that spirit.

There is a mountain not far from where I live. She is called Mount Tamalpais, which means "sleeping maiden" in the language of the first people here. She looks like a maiden who is lying down. When I go to visit that mountain, it is always an emotional experience. I'm not upset, and there is nothing presently threatening her. It's just that I love that mountain, and it is so beautiful to look out at the world while standing on her forehead. When I feel afraid or need help of any kind, I call on her. I imagine her in my heart, and then I have courage. I ask her to tell me the truth, and she always does. She is my guide, and I talk with her as easily as I talk with my own mother. I am talking with a mountain, something you are not supposed to be able to do, yet I know that it's real.

If the plants and trees can have spirits and can talk with us, why not the rest of nature? According to the new cosmology, there is no reason. Where you are right now, whether it is in a city with high-rise buildings, in a desert, in suburbia, by a lake — the place where you are right now has a spirit, feelings, and a voice. Engage with the spirit of your place and of any place on earth where you go. Recognize it, appreciate it, honor it, talk to it, and ask it to be in alliance with you. See what happens.

EXERCISES: PLANTS AND THE LANDSCAPE

There are a lot of exercises in this section. Do the ones that appeal to you. The process for talking with a plant, a tree, or a mountain is the same as the process for talking with animals. To review the techniques for focusing and connecting, refer to pages 129–130 in chapter 8.

Exercise 1: Who's Touching Whom?

Spend some time sitting with your back up against a tree, or holding a rock in your hand, or placing your hand on a flower or on the earth. Focus on the idea that the tree or rock or plant you are feeling also feels you — it actually feels you touching it. There is a spirit and consciousness there that is just as aware of you as you are of it. Ask if the one you are touching has anything to tell you.

Exercise 2: Singing

It's been my experience that the beings of nature love it when we sing to them, even if we're off key. When you are out gardening or hiking or hanging out in nature, try singing or humming. You could make up a song for a particular being — a song for the wind, or a song for the dogwood tree — or you can sing a song you know. When you're finished, ask how they liked it.

Exercise 3: Appreciation

Talk with the plants in your garden or the trees in the park or the wild plants you meet on a hike. Tell them why you appreciate them. Explain the meaning they have for you in your life. Tell them what you hope and dream for them. Ask if they have anything to tell you.

Exercise 4: Healing

Talk with a plant (or a tree) that is sick or dying. Use your intuition to scan the plant and determine what is wrong and what is needed. Send energy healing if the plant wants it. Send love. If there is any hope that the plant could recover, imagine it whole and happy and thriving. Send that image and feeling to the plant. Do this every day, and see what happens.

Exercise 5: Honoring

Create a ceremony to honor some aspect of nature. For example, you could honor a creek in your area by pouring a small offering of honey into the creek and telling the creek why you honor it. Or honor a tree by making an altar or leaving a gift of food, an herb, or something sweet, and then tell the tree why you honor it.

When you eat a meal, save a small portion to give back to the earth to honor her.

Honor whatever being you wish to by making an offering and telling the being why you honor it.

Exercise 6: Talking with Plants and Pests

Interview a plant or tree. Take the role of a reporter. Ask questions about its life and feelings. Ask biological questions that you can later verify. Ask if the plant or tree has a question for you.

If you are experiencing an overabundance of pests, talk with them. Ask the insects not to destroy the plants. Find out why there is an infestation and what can you do to help make the plant more vigorous. Offer to share what you have — some for the insects, some for you. Strike deals. If you have too many weeds, ask them if they could back off a little and stop taking over the yard. Find out if there is some agreement you can make with the weeds to coexist. Tell them how much you would appreciate their cooperation. See what happens.

Exercise 7: Working with the Spirits

Greet the spirits of the plants and of the land where you live. Tell them how much you appreciate them. If there is something you need or want for the plants or for the place, ask the nature spirits to help you with that. Make an offering (grain, seeds, sweets) to honor the nature spirits. If you wish, you may create an altar to recognize the spirit of your place and create your own ritual for honoring this spirit.

Exercise 8: Know and Protect Your Bioregion

Learn about your bioregion — the natural environment and ecosystems of your local area. Where does your water come from? Study the animal and plant populations. Learn about the ecology of your area before it was urbanized or converted to single-crop agriculture. What happened there? What lived there formerly? Track the migrations of the animals in your bioregion. Search for the native plants that are left. Stay in touch with all of them. Join with other people in your area to protect and restore your bioregion.

Exercise 9: Find Your Ally in Nature

Finding your ally among the plants and the landscape may take some time. You need to visit with the plants and go to different landscapes and pay attention. Which being feels like an ally to you? Does one particular flower, herb, tree, or feature of the landscape keep calling you back to visit? Once you feel you have found your ally, ask for any help and advice you seek. Ask for your ally's spirit name.

Exercise 10: The Landscape and the Elements

You can talk with any aspect of nature, including any location in nature. You can talk with lakes, creeks, rivers, ponds, the ocean, and the rain. You can talk with land formations, like mountains, rocks, and the soil. You can talk with the wind and with fire. You can interview these aspects of nature in the same way you interviewed an animal. You may find, like I did with the mountain, that some aspect of nature takes on a special significance in your life.

Chapter Sixteen

Collaborating with the Earth

During one of my classes, I read aloud a passage about how all the animals and beings of the natural world want humans to learn to reconnect and communicate with them so that we can work together to save the planet. After I finished reading, my dog Brydie, who was sitting next to me on the couch, carefully laid her head against my heart and closed her eyes. She stayed that way for a long time, as we watched, transfixed. She has never done that before or since. She was telling me that she totally agreed with the words I had read and wanted this change to come about.

I believe that other life forms are aware of what's happening on the earth and know that it is deadly serious. They are waiting for us to collaborate with them, and they do want us to reconnect and do something to stop the destruction. But humans are good at pretending that bad things aren't happening when they really are — especially now, when we are confronted by such a vast number of seemingly insoluble problems.

WHAT TO DO?

I don't know what to do, and I don't have the solutions. But I am sure of this: The way we do everything has to change. The way we grow food, the materials we use from the earth, and the ways in which we earn our living, get around, entertain ourselves, do business, share power, distribute wealth, resolve conflict, and coexist with each other (men and women and different races, cultures, and species) have got to change all around the world. Otherwise, we will destroy ourselves and life on our planet fairly soon.

The things that people are doing now to stop the destruction of the earth are good, but the opposing forces are very strong and there are too few people actively working to turn things around.

Theodore Rozak,[1] a proponent of ecopsychology,[2] says that at a deep, unconscious level, most of us are grieving about what is happening to the earth and to nature, and that we do not want it to be happening. To cope with those feelings, most of us have gone into denial. To avoid feeling the pain, we pretend that nothing is happening to the earth and that what we do causes no harm. But pretending that nothing is happening, as Derrick Jensen points out in his compelling book, *A Language Older Than Words,*[3] only makes things worse and leaves us incapable of action.

It is very difficult to stay conscious. Environmental activists know this better than anyone because they put themselves at the front lines of the destruction of nature. Activist and songwriter David Grimes, who lives in Prince William Sound in Alaska, witnessed the destruction of life in the Sound following the Exxon Valdez oil spill. I recently spoke with him about how people cope with being activists for the earth. He relayed the following story told to him by an activist friend.4

After years of tree-sitting and other nonviolent protesting against clear-cutting, the woman found herself totally angry and grief-stricken. These feelings were overwhelming every aspect of her life and she was alienating her friends and family. She told David that one day, when she found herself crying in a grove of trees slated to be clear-cut, she felt the trees communicating with her. What she received came mainly as feelings that seemed to be coming from the trees to her. The essence of the message was that the trees did not want her to sacrifice herself for them. They considered her their ally and wanted her to remain strong and balanced so that she could continue to be their voice in the world. This experience shifted the way she approached her activist work, and after that she was able to come to terms with the enormous pain incurred by being an activist and staying in touch with the distress of the planet. It was as if the condemned trees imparted some kind of grace to this woman before they were struck down.

Perhaps one way to cope with the overwhelming emotions we may have about the earth — the emotions that send us into the false protection of denial — is to do what that activist did: Talk with the nonhumans on this earth about the situation we are in. We may find the same kind of strength that she found to go through our painful emotions and emerge able to help without being overwhelmed.

The nonhumans of our world are telling us this message: "Don't abandon us; don't shut us out." I suspect that, as things get worse, more of us will see that being in denial isn't working. It is clear to me that we need, instead, to join together around the world to oppose what is happening, until our numbers and our commitment outweigh the strength of the global corporations and superpower governments that are destroying the earth.

Ideas for Collaboration

I started this book with the story of the U'wa, a tribe of people who live in the cloud forests of the Colombian Andes. As you will recall, when their tribal lands were threatened by oil exploration, the U'wa decided to talk to the oil and tell it to "move" and hide from the oil company drills. After they did this, Occidental Petroleum, the multinational oil company doing the exploratory drilling, announced that it was giving up its efforts at oil exploration; they had been unable to locate the large reserves of oil initially identified on the land.[5] I suspect that the U'wa thought a long time before they came up with that idea. I have been wondering, "What else can we do like that?" What if we convinced *all* the oil in the world to hide? Then we'd be forced to do what we should be doing anyway: shifting to vegetable diesel, methane, wind, solar, and hydrogen power — *renewable* sources of energy. Converting to renewable energy is totally feasible, and we'd be doing it today all over the world if the petrochemical conglomerates weren't blocking the way. So far that's the only idea I have come up with, but I am going to keep working on it.

What follows are some suggestions I've collected for collaborating with the earth. These techniques involve visualizations and methods for shifting energy. I am not including suggestions for direct actions like protests, lawsuits, and tree-sitting. You hear enough about those actions from other sources. But their omission here does not diminish their importance. I am suggesting that you do the energy work in addition to direct actions, not instead of them. We need to become visionary activists and collaborate to turn things around on both the physical and the spiritual planes.

You Are What You Imagine

In her book *Making the Gods Work for You,*[6] Caroline Casey counsels that we will get what we focus on. She encourages us to imagine what we truly want to have happen in our lives and on the earth, no matter how implausible. To do this, imagine what you want as if it were already happening. Make it as vivid as possible. Close your eyes and use all your senses. Imagine it as if you were watching a movie. Do this often, especially when you find yourself dwelling on the negative.

Ritual

Our ancestors used ritual to encourage the rain to fall and the crops to grow. They asked for all kinds of help from the elements, the spirits of place, and the animals and plants. Make up your own rituals to ask for what you want. For example, ask the wind to bring a change of heart to all humans. Then blow a handful of cornmeal into the wind as an offering to speed it on its task.

Dream a New World

Your dreams have power. Aborigines believe that dreamtime is the real time. Use your dreams to change things. Casey suggests that, before you go to sleep, think of something you want to accomplish or something you want to see happen. Ask aloud that this thing come to pass. As you sleep, the thought will go out into the world and become manifest. You can also ask to receive guidance in your dream. To do this you ask for what you want right before you go to sleep. Be as specific as possible. Then have pen and paper near your bed, so that when you awaken you can jot down whatever you recall.

Spirit Talk

If you are having a problem with someone, talk with this person spirit to spirit. To do this, imagine meeting with them in a safe and protected place in nature. You may also invite your guides to come in to protect you. Close your eyes and see yourself in this place. Imagine having a conversation, from your heart, with this person. Say everything you have not been able to say in real life and explain what you want. Listen to the person's responses. End the conversation when you wish. Realize that some people are completely unable to do things differently, even though their actions are causing great harm. Ask the universe to send healing to such persons and to bring forth whatever is necessary to remedy the situation caused by these people. Now see the person walking away from you. Then you can leave and return to your body and normal consciousness.

Prayer

In her book *Medicine for the Earth*,[7] Sandra Ingerman tells a story about some Tibetan Buddhist monks who came to Southern California many years ago when there had been a prediction of a major earthquake. People in Los Angeles were beginning to panic; some were even leaving the city. The monks came to pray for the land. She said the message they brought was that, when there is trouble, the best thing to do is to gather with others and pray. The expected earthquake did not come. Who knows whether the monks helped divert it?

Spend five minutes a day praying for the changes you want to see on the earth and in your life. Try to do this at the same time every day so that it becomes a habit. You might also form a prayer group with others. Working together to pray will be more powerful.

Healing

Using the techniques described for healing animals in chapter 12, send healing to the places on earth that need it. Do this as a daily practice and try doing it in a group to increase the intensity.

Now That You Can Hear, Listen

If I did my job well, you should be able to hear the voices of nature. Now you can go out and find those animals, plants, and places who are your guides. When you find them, ask them what you should do. Ask how you can best help at this time — when nothing less than the fate of the world is at stake. Ask a river otter, a valley oak tree, a gray fox, the ocean, a dragonfly, a marsh hawk, a horsetail fern, a snowy plover, a badger, a nuthatch, a slender salamander, a bat, a hummingbird, a lady's slipper, a dolphin, a cottontail, a pond turtle, a buckeye tree, a golden eagle, a waterfall, a rattlesnake, a tree frog, a thimbleberry bush, or a mountain of stone. Now that you can hear, go out and listen.

Answer Key

CHAPTER SIX

All the animals in the photographs are mine. I have tried to think of every facet of each animal's personality and everything that each one likes and dislikes. However, there are bound to be some things I left out. If what you get isn't on this list, please do not count it as wrong. Instead mark it as unknown; I may have just left it off the list. When you calculate your percentage of right answers, leave these unknown answers out of the calculations. Also, if you get something about personality that turns up listed in the likes or dislikes section, count it as a correct answer.

Hazel

Age: Seventeen years old as of 2002.

Personality: smart, agile, mischievous, inventive, jealous, creative, stuck up, clever, profound. She has a healthy ego, loves to play games, and helps me with writing. She is a thinker, a good hunter (though she doesn't do it much anymore), a good communicator, a big help to her person, basically friendly to other cats if they are nice, and less trusting of dogs, but if they are nice she will be OK. She likes to be admired and be the center of attention.

Likes: playing chase, teasing dogs, watching from up high, going on the roof, making people laugh, being kissed, playing with toys, sleeping in comfy chairs and on big pillows, warm lamps and heat lamps, warm blankets, sleeping right next to my head, tearing up paper, sitting in the in-box on my desk, knocking things off my dresser, visitors, helping people learn animal communication, meeting me when I come home, running through the house and going nuts, being admired, being called princess, exploring, canned food (tuna and chicken), raw food, dry crunchy kibbles, cantaloupe, cheese, butter, asparagus tips, and having her stomach, back, ears, and chin rubbed.

Dislikes: the Siamese cat across the street, having her nails clipped (except by one specific vet), some dogs (especially loud, noisy ones), being ignored, my new kitten Tule (she's a little jealous), being held for too long, getting in the car, the vacuum cleaner, getting old, getting stiff, loud noises.

Brydie

Age: Seven years old as of 2002.

Personality: very high energy, athletic, quick in every way, nervous, easily upset, friendly, curious, excitable, easily distracted, easily scared, sweet and cuddly. She is a busybody, tends toward insecurity, has abuse in her past, is a picky eater, and has a good sense of humor. She smiles a lot (I have trained her to smile). She has to be the alpha dog with other dogs and will get a bit pushy at first, but then likes to play and settle down.

Likes: chasing cats, following cats around, watching cats, digging up gophers, digging in dirt, sleeping on the bed, going for walks, cuddling, being off the leash, running, playing with other dogs, chasing a ball (or anything), tearing up paper, sitting on the furniture, going to the fields and in the marsh, going to the ocean and the lake, going anywhere in the car, treats, and her food (veggies, raw meat, and bones, as well as cookies, cheese, potatoes, and eggs). Her friends are Max (a big white dog), Marmalade (an orange cat, now dead), Hazel, Tule (my new tabby cat), Bear (my black male dog), and Dougal (my big brown male dog who recently died).

Dislikes: Jenny (my older cat), having Jenny approach her anywhere, being disturbed when sleeping, going to the vet (except that she likes to see the cats there), getting her nails trimmed, loud noises, angry people, baths, collars and leashes, my going away.

Dylan

Age: Twenty-one years old as of 2002.

Personality: Mostly calm, smart, thoughtful, kind, lovable, not too pushy, compassionate, happy, content, and not much into working. He has a good sense of humor, does not like to fight, is stoic, is the bottom horse in a herd, loves creature comforts, and loves to play. He can be a little stubborn and a little impatient. He is trained to voice commands and is usually very cooperative.

Likes: chasing and playing with dogs and other horses, playing chase with people, alfalfa, sugar cubes, anything sweet, carrots, medicinal herbs, grain, horse feeds, going for walks, being in a big pasture, being in a herd, being warm, lying down at night on something soft, sightseeing, eating grass, being groomed, having the inside of his ears scratched, being massaged, having people visit, talking with people, making people laugh, teaching people to communicate.

Dislikes: cats on his back, dogs who chase him, pigs of any sort, shots, sore feet, being sick, going in trailers (somewhat), moving to new places, being in the rain, being alone, horse blankets, being away from other horses, being around mean people or sad horses, weird noises, cold-water baths (has to be warm), being adjusted by the chiropractor, taking medicine orally from a syringe.

Scoring

For each animal, add up your total correct answers. If you got something about likes or dislikes and it was on the personality list instead, count it as a correct answer. Now add up your number of incorrect answers, omitting those answers that were not on the list. (These answers may be correct.)

To calculate your accuracy percentage, add the number of incorrect answers to the number of correct answers to come up the total possible points for that animal. For example, if you had twenty correct and eight incorrect answers, your total would be twenty-eight. Then the percentage of correct answers would be:

Per the example: There are 20 correct answers and the total number of answers (correct plus incorrect) is 28.

20 times 100 percent divided by 28 = 71 percent

The accuracy rate for this example would be 71 percent.

CHAPTER SEVEN

Exercise 2: Practice on a Person

My likes: singing, hiking, swimming, bird-watching, horse-back riding, camping, gardening, travel, children, most kinds of music, dancing, mystery novels, reading, movies, shopping, cleaning, snakes, almost anything alternative, environmental protection, and sustainability.

My dislikes: crowds, noise, shopping malls, fast food, celery, okra, peas, off-road vehicles, mean or conceited people, TV, cooking, some spiders, commercialized anything, right-wing politics, golf, bowling.

Exercise 3: Try Again with an Animal

Bear

Age: Two years old as of 2002.

Personality: curious, happy, calm, smart, easily distracted. He is a quick learner, very friendly to all people but a good guard dog, very nice to cats, and friendly to all dogs but prefers people. He really gets in your face.

Likes: food, treats, people, kids, other dogs, running races with other dogs, eating poop, going for walks, howling and barking, having his tummy and ears scratched, giving kisses, jumping up on the table, sleeping on the tabletop, keeping watch from the tabletop, eating the cat's food, rummaging in the garbage, making people happy, meeting new people. He also likes rolling in dead, smelly things and chasing horses, bikes, and joggers (but doesn't get the opportunity).

Dislikes: loud noises, hearing people yell or get mad, being tied up, being around mean dogs, being attacked by dogs, cats coming up to his face, being pulled by his collar, not getting dinner on time, not getting enough food, bathing, not going for a walk every day.

Chapter Eight

Exercise 1: Do You Like...? (Marta)

Skydiving: While I might think that skydiving is a neat idea, and it would be great if I could do it, I would never have the courage to try; it is way too scary.

Cooking: Not really. I would much rather have someone else do the cooking. I'll do the washing up.

Going to my high-school reunion: I never have gone. For the longest time I thought, "Yech, not for me." But lately I have been thinking that it might actually be intriguing. If the impressions you got were ambivalent, that's why.

Getting up early: I like to get up early; I am often up before the sun.

Swimming in the ocean: I have done it and liked it, but only in warm water and shallow areas. I would not like swimming in a cold, dark ocean.

Licorice: I like it.

Exercise 2: Do You Like...? (Brydie)

Going in the water: Brydie tends to run through water. She is always on the go. She will run through puddles and creeks. Lakes are a bit different; I tried to get her to swim with me in a lake one time and she got scared. Swimming in deep water is not something she would go for. She might go after a stick in the water, but probably not a ball. She would not be eager to go swimming out to the middle of anything. At the beach, she likes to run through the edge of the surf, but she is not one to go crashing into the waves — though she did do that one time when some friends took her surfing with them.

Children: When I first got Brydie, she was afraid of children. I had to teach her that they were OK. She is curious about infants and toddlers, and likes the way they smell and likes to lick them. But she can get a little spooked when they wave their hands around or come at her. With older kids who know how to act around dogs, she is great. She gives them kisses, likes to smell them, and is friendly. She thinks little boys can be fun to play with, but usually trusts little girls more. When we are out on walks, she would much rather run through the fields than visit any of the children we meet.

Carrots as treats: Not particularly interested.

Being brushed and combed: She is not overly fond of being brushed or combed. She just puts up with it.

Chapter Notes

INTRODUCTION

1   T. C. McLuhan, ed., *Touch the Earth: A Self-Portrait of Indian Existence* (New York: Simon & Schuster, 1971), p. 15.
2   McLuhan, *Touch the Earth,* p. 23.
3   Rainforest Action Network (RAN) Web page (www.ran.org). (You can visit the RAN Web site to find out more about the U'wa and help them in their campaign.)
4   Gabrielle Banks, "Columbian Tribe Topples Mighty Oil Giant," www.alternet.org, May 6, 2002.

CHAPTER ONE

1   Boone's essays were published posthumously as *Adventures in Kinship with All Life* (Joshua Tree, Calif.: Tree of Life Publications, 1990).
2   On a vision quest, a tradition common to many native cultures, the quester travels alone into nature to seek vision and guidance. Usually

there is a period of fasting; sometimes participants go without water for several days.

3   Frank Walters, *Book of the Hopi* (New York: Viking Press, 1963).

CHAPTER TWO

1   Belleruth Naparstek, *Your Sixth Sense: Activating Your Psychic Potential* (New York: HarperCollins, 1997).

2   Russell Targ and Keith Harary, *The Mind Race: Understanding and Using Psychic Ability* (New York: Random House, 1984).

3   Russell Targ and Jane Katra, Ph.D., *Miracles of the Mind: Exploring Nonlocal Consciousness and Spiritual Healing* (Novato, Calif.: New World Library, 1999), p. 61.

4   Ibid., p. 27.

5   Christian de Quincey, *Radical Nature: Rediscovering the Soul of Matter* (Montpelier, Vt.: Invisible Cities Press, 2002).

6   Gary Schwartz, Ph.D., *The Afterlife Experiments: Breakthrough Scientific Evidence of Life after Death* (New York: Pocket Books, 2002).

7   Kirstin Miller, "The Afterlife Experiments: An Interview with Dr. Gary Schwartz," *Psychic Reader,* vol. 27, no. 6, June 2002, pp. 8-10, 13.

8   David Abram, *The Spell of the Sensuous: Perception and Language in a More-Than-Human World* (New York: Pantheon, 1996).

9   Marija Gimbutas, *The Language of the Goddess* (San Francisco: Harper-Collins, 1989). Also see Joan Marler, ed., *From the Realm of the Ancestors: An Anthology in Honor of Marija Gimbutas* (Manchester, Conn.: Knowledge, Ideas and Trends, 1997).

10 I didn't realize until I read Linda Kohanov's *The Tao of Equus: A Woman's Journey of Healing and Transformation through the Way of the Horse* (Novato, Calif.: New World Library, 2001) that there was popular controversy about Gimbutas's theory. In her book, Kohanov dismisses the idea of this invasion of Kurdish horsemen based on her assessment of the Kurdish culture. She feels it is unlikely that the Kurds would have done such a thing and ascribes the shift from the goddess religions to patriarchy as being the result of the rise of settled agriculture. Kohanov is concerned that nomadic horse cultures not be stereotyped as destructive and patriarchal, and that is a good point. She is also concerned that the horse not be blamed for the fall of the goddess societies, the idea being that without horses the invaders might not have been so successful. I share her concern about that; I love horses and

don't want them to be the bad guys of prehistory. However, if one studies the body of Gimbutas's work and the excellent archeological data contained in Marler's work, *From the Realm of the Ancestors,* the data are pretty conclusive. Through the analysis of artifacts, architecture, radiocarbon dating, and DNA testing, it is evident that there was an invading culture from the north that superseded the prevailing cultures of Old Europe. Settled agriculture persisted for thousands of years within the goddess cultures of Old Europe. These cultures were only destroyed when exposed to the marauding or patriarchal culture that came from the north. I don't think one needs to paint all of the nomadic horse cultures with the same brush, but it seems undeniable based on the archeological evidence that at least some faction of this culture went amok sometime about 7,000 years ago.

11 Monica Sjoo, *Return of the Dark/Light Mother or New Age Armageddon?* (Austin, Tex.: Plain View Press, 1999), p. 102.

12 Christian de Quincey, *Radical Nature: Rediscovering the Soul of Matter* (Montpelier, Vt.: Invisible Cities Press, 2002), p. 5.

13 Jeffrey Moussaieff Masson and Susan McCarthy, *When Elephants Weep: The Emotional Lives of Animals* (New York: Delacorte Press, 1995).

14 Charles Darwin, *The Expression of Emotions in Man and Animals* (1872; reprint, Chicago: University of Chicago Press, 1965).

15 Margot Lasher, *And The Animals Will Teach You: Discovering Ourselves through Our Relationships with Animals* (New York: Berkeley Books, 1996).

16 Rupert Sheldrake, *Dogs That Know When Their Owners Are Coming Home: And Other Unexplained Powers of Animals* (New York: Crown Publishers, 1999).

CHAPTER THREE

1 The researchers referenced in this book are:

Christian de Quincey, *Radical Nature: Rediscovering the Soul of Matter* (Montpelier, Vt.: Invisible Cities Press, 2002).

Gary Schwartz, Ph.D., *The Afterlife Experiments: Breakthrough Scientific Evidence of Life after Death* (New York: Pocket Books, 2002).

Rupert Sheldrake, *Dogs That Know When Their Owners Are Coming Home: And Other Unexplained Powers of Animals* (New York: Crown Publishers, 1999).

Russell Targ and Keith Harary, *The Mind Race: Understanding and Using Psychic Ability* (New York: Random House, 1984).

Russell Targ and Jane Katra, Ph.D., *Miracles of the Mind: Exploring*

Nonlocal Consciousness and Spiritual Healing (Novato, Calif.: New World Library, 1999).

2 Rupert Sheldrake, *Dogs That Know When Their Owners Are Coming Home: And Other Unexplained Powers of Animals* (New York: Crown Publishers, 1999).

3 The method I use is to simply physically sweep my body with my hands and pull the phantom feeling out of wherever it has become lodged. If I have a sensation of tightness in my throat, I pull that feeling out of my throat area and then flick it off my fingertips to the ground. I imagine this energy being recycled by the earth, like composting.

CHAPTER FOUR

1 Marta Williams, "What's on Your Horse's Mind?" *Whole Horse Journal,* vol. 3, no. 3, May/June 1998, pp. 14–16. The story about Red was written up in the same journal: Pat Miller, "A Bad Horse or One in Pain?" *Whole Horse Journal,* vol. 4, no. 1, January/February 1999, p. 13.

2 Rupert Sheldrake, *Dogs That Know When Their Owners Are Coming Home: And Other Unexplained Powers of Animals* (New York: Crown Publishers, 1999).

3 Mona Lisa Schultz, *Awakening Intuition: Using Your Mind-Body Network for Insight and Healing* (New York: Harmony Books, 1998), pp. 323–327.

4 To learn more, read McMoneagle's book *Remote Viewing Secrets: A Handbook* (Charlottesville, Va.: Hampton Roads Publishing Company, 2000), p. 167. Also visit the Web site of the Time Service Department, United States Naval Observatory, http://tycho.usno.navy.mil/sidereal.

5 Dean Radin, *The Conscious Universe: The Scientific Truth of Psychic Phenomena* (New York: HarperCollins, 1997).
Web site for remote viewing: www.remote-viewing.com/
Web site for James Spottiswoode & Associates:
www.jsasoc.com/docs/isseem.pdf

CHAPTER FIVE

1 "There's a Real Cat Burglar on the Prowl," *The Evening Telegram,* Mattawa, Ontario, August 22, 1998, p. 7.

2 Flower essences are just water that contains the "essence" of a flower. When the flower essence is made, the flower is placed in the water for a specified time and then removed. There is no botanical component in the

water. The essence is then preserved using a little alcohol or some other agent. Flower essences work on a vibrational level, affecting the emotional body. Although it doesn't seem logical that they could have any impact, many people who use them for themselves and their animals swear by them. As far as I'm concerned, using flower essences is a cheap experiment; it can't hurt and it might help. There are many different kinds of essences. Please refer to my suggested reading and resource sections for recommendations. You can also look for books at your local bookstore and herb store, or search the Web for the term "flower essences."

CHAPTER SEVEN

1   Mona Lisa Schultz, *Awakening Intuition: Using Your Mind-Body Network for Insight and Healing* (New York: Harmony Books, 1998), pp. 331–337.
2   Karen Pryor, *Don't Shoot the Dog: The New Art of Teaching and Training* (New York: Bantam Books, 1984).

CHAPTER EIGHT

1   Pete Sanders, Jr., *You Are Psychic: The Free Soul Method* (New York: Fawcett Columbine Book, 1989).
2   Belleruth Naparstek, *Your Sixth Sense: Activating Your Psychic Potential* (New York: HarperCollins, 1997), p. 110.

CHAPTER ELEVEN

1   Martin Goldstein, D.V.M. *The Nature of Animal Healing: The Path to Your Pet's Health, Happiness, and Longevity* (New York: Knopf, 1999), pp. 281–302.

CHAPTER TWELVE

1   To find out more about holistic care for animals, see the resources and suggested reading sections.
2   See Larry Dossey's Web site: www.dosseydossey.com.
3   Martin Goldstein, D.V.M. *The Nature of Animal Healing: The Path to Your Pet's Health, Happiness, and Longevity* (New York: Knopf, 1999), pp. 71–104.
4   For example, leaking underground storage tanks from old gas stations have contaminated groundwater aquifers across the United States with carcinogenic chemicals such as benzene. Pesticides can also seep into groundwater and end up in drinking water.

5   Goldstein, *The Nature of Animal Healing,* pp. 43–70.

6   One thing to research is tofu; I don't recommend using tofu as a meat substitute. After being a vegetarian for many years and eating a lot of tofu, I am now certain that it is not a healthy food. To learn more about the hidden dangers of eating soy products, read the following article on Dr. Joseph Mercola's Web site, www.mercola.com/article/soy. A raw, whole-food diet for a dog can be designed to avoid all the typical foods that animals (and people) can be allergic too, including wheat, corn, soy, cow's milk, sugar, and yeast. However, going completely vegetarian can end up increasing the animal's exposure to these potentially unhealthy foods.

7   There are serious ethical issues about using animals for meat or dairy products. Animals raised commercially are tortured; there is no other way to describe what happens to them. We all need to stop supporting the meat and dairy industries. On the other hand, there is the issue of whether our carnivorous pets can be healthy without eating meat. There are also people's individual dietary needs and preferences. My personal opinion is that we need to work on creating humane farming as the first goal; we need to educate people to purchase only organic, humanely raised and slaughtered animals. At the same time, we need to encourage people to eat less meat and fewer dairy products. I was a vegetarian for twenty years, and I got pretty sick from that diet. At this point, I don't eat any cow cheese or milk, but I do use cow butter and sheep and goat cheese, all from organic, free-range animals. I also eat free-range chicken and eggs, and I feed meat to my animals. I am contemplating raising the chickens that I intend to use for food. That way, I will know that they had a decent life and as humane a death as I could arrange. I realize that some people will see a conflict in my being an animal communicator and eating meat. I can only say that maybe it's the biologist in me coming out. Lots of animals eat other animals. I fed animals to animals for six years when I worked in wildlife rehabilitation. The hawks, owls, foxes, badgers, coyotes, and seals I took care of would have died if I had not fed them meat and fish. I don't see the eating part as the biggest problem, except for the fact that humans are so grossly overpopulating the earth that our meat-eating habits have enormous negative impacts. I am concerned about that problem, and about our overfishing the oceans and about the misery, torture, and cruel deaths that animals endure in the meat industry. I don't think I will personally be able to get away

from any of that unless I raise the animals myself, so that's the direction I'm headed in.

8   Diana Thompson, "Alfalfa: More Harm Than Good?" *Whole Horse Journal,* vol. 2, no. 5, September/October 1997, pp. 6–8.

9   It would be good to consult the animal about this, too, although I typically find that the animal has no preference.

CHAPTER THIRTEEN

1   To find out how to use a pendulum or a dowsing rod, you can do a search on the Internet or consult books that will instruct you. Check the online bookstores or your local metaphysical bookstore.

CHAPTER FOURTEEN

1   I think of many domesticated but untamed animals as being essentially wild.

2   J. Allen Boone, *Adventures in Kinship with All Life* (Joshua Tree, Calif.: Tree of Life Publications, 1990).

3   For more information on attracting wildlife to your yard, visit the Web site for the National Wildlife Federation (www.nwf.org).

4   Joanne Elizabeth Lauck, *The Voice of the Infinite in the Small: Revisioning the Insect-Human Connection* (Mill Spring, N.C.: Granite Publications, 1998).

5   For example, installation of a sand barrier under your house denies termites entry and circumvents the use of pesticides. Also, some of my clients tell me that geese are great deterrents to curious rattlesnakes. There are many books on the subject of nontoxic pest control. Check the Internet, the local library, an organic nursery, and your local ecology center.

6   Buffie Johnson, *Lady of the Beasts: The Goddess and Her Sacred Animals* (Rochester, Vt.: Inner Traditions International, 1994).

7   Dianne Skafte, Ph.D., *When Oracles Speak: Understanding the Signs and Symbols All around Us* (Wheaton, Ill.: Quest Books, 2000).

CHAPTER FIFTEEN

1   Peter Tompkins and Christopher Bird, *The Secret Life of Plants* (New York: HarperCollins, 1973).

2   Tompkins and Bird, *The Secret Life of Plants,* pp. 127–134.

3   Russell Targ and Jane Katra, Ph.D., *Miracles of the Mind: Exploring Nonlocal Consciousness and Spiritual Healing* (Novato, Calif.: New World Library, 1999).

4   Christian De Quincey, *Radical Nature: Rediscovering the Soul of Matter* (Montpelier, Vt.: Invisible Cities Press, 2002).

5   Rupert Sheldrake, *Dogs That Know When Their Owners Are Coming Home: And Other Unexplained Powers of Animals* (New York: Crown Publishers, 1999).

6   Dean Radin, *The Conscious Universe: The Scientific Truth of Psychic Phenomena* (New York: HarperCollins, 1997).

7   Tompkins and Bird, *The Secret Life of Plants*, pp. 17–31.

8   Tompkins and Bird, *The Secret Life of Plants*, p. 361–373. Do also read Monica Sjoo's book *Return of the Dark/Light Mother or New Age Armageddon?* (Austin, Tex.: Plain View Press, 1999), to get a different perspective on Findhorn.

9   Stephen Harrod Buhner, *The Lost Language of Plants: The Ecological Importance of Plant Medicines to Life on Earth* (White River Junction, Vt.: Chelsea Green Publishing, 2002), pp. 258–259.

10 Buhner, *The Lost Language of Plants*, pp. 80–82.

11 To find out more about flower essences, see the resources and suggested reading sections at the back of this book.

12 Julia Butterfly Hill, *The Legacy of Luna: The Story of a Tree, a Woman, and the Struggle to Save the Redwoods* (San Francisco: HarperSanFrancisco, 2001).

CHAPTER SIXTEEN

1   Theodore Rozak, *The Voice of the Earth: An Exploration of Ecopsychology* (Grand Rapids, Mich.: Phanes Press, Inc., 2001).

2   Ecopsychology is the study of the relationship between the natural environment, the state of the earth and nature, and the human psyche. It is a relatively obscure field because, like the new cosmology, widespread adherence to its tenets would require a complete revision of a current system — in this case, the mental health system.

3   Derrick Jensen, *A Language Older Than Words* (New York: Context Books, 2000).

4   Personal conversation with David Grimes, July 5, 2002.

5   Gabrielle Banks, "Colombian Tribe Topples Mighty Oil Giant," May 6, 2002, www.alternet.org.

6   Caroline Casey, *Making the Gods Work for You: The Astrological Language of the Psyche* (New York: Three Rivers Press, 1998).

7   Sandra Ingerman, *Medicine for the Earth: How to Transform Personal and Environmental Toxins* (New York: Three Rivers Press, 2000).

Suggested Reading

Books by Animal Communicators

Boone, J. Allen. *Kinship with All Life.* New York: Harper & Brothers, 1954.

———. *Adventures in Kinship with all Life.* Joshua Tree, Calif.: Tree of Life Publications, 1990.

Fitzpatrick, Sonya and Patricia Burkhart Smith. *What the Animals Tell Me.* New York: Hyperion, 1997.

Gurney, Carol. *The Language of the Animals: 7 Steps to Communicating with Animals.* New York: Dell Publishing, 2001.

Hiby, Lydia and Bonnie Weintraub. *Conversations with Animals: Cherished Messages and Memories As Told by an Animal Communicator.* Troutdale, Oreg.: NewSage Press, 1998.

Kinkade, Amelia. *Straight from the Horse's Mouth: How to Talk to Animals and Get Answers.* New York: Crown Publishers, 2001.

Lydecker, Beatrice. *Stories the Animals Tell Me.* Self-published, 1986.

———. *What the Animals Tell Me.* New York: Harper & Row, 1989.

MacKay, Nicci. *Spoken in Whispers: The Autobiography of a Horse Whisperer.* New York: Fireside, 1997.

Smith, Penelope. *Animal Talk: Interspecies Telepathic Communication.* Hillsboro, Oreg.: Beyond Words Publishing Company, 1999.

Summers, Patty. *Talking with the Animals.* Charlottesville, Va.: Hampton Roads Publishing Company, Inc., 1998.

INTUITIVE ABILITY, COMMUNICATION, AND CONNECTION

Casey, Caroline. *Making the Gods Work for You: The Astrological Language of the Psyche.* New York: Three Rivers Press, 1998.

Chernak McElroy, Susan. *Animals As Teachers and Healers: True Stories and Reflections.* Troutdale, Oreg.: NewSage Press, 1996.

Choquette, Sonia. *The Psychic Pathway: A Workbook for Reawakening the Voice of Your Soul.* New York: Crown Publishers, 1995.

Graff, Dale. *Tracks in the Psychic Wilderness: An Exploration of Remote Viewing, ESP, Precognitive Dreaming and Synchronicity.* Boston: Element Books, 1998.

Knapp, Caroline. *Pack of Two: The Intricate Bond between People and Dogs.* New York: Dell Publishing, 1998.

Kohanov, Linda. *The Tao of Equus: A Woman's Journey of Healing and Transformation through the Way of the Horse.* Novato, Calif.: New World Library, 2001.

Lasher, Margot. *And the Animals Will Teach You: Discovering Ourselves through Our Relationships with Animals.* New York: Berkeley Books, 1996.

Lauck, Joanne Elizabeth. *The Voice of the Infinite in the Small: Revisioning the Insect-Human Connection.* Mill Spring, N.C.: Granite Publications, 1998.

Masson, Jeffrey Moussaieff and Susan McCarthy. *When Elephants Weep: The Emotional Lives of Animals.* New York: Delacorte Press, 1995.

Myers, Arthur. *Communicating with Animals: The Spiritual Connection Between People and Animals.* Chicago: Contemporary Books, 1997.

Naparstek, Belleruth. *Your Sixth Sense: Activating Your Psychic Potential.* New York: HarperCollins, 1997.

Ostrander, Sheila and Lynn Schroeder. *Psychic Discoveries Behind the Iron Curtain.* Englewood Cliffs, N.J.: Prentice-Hall, Inc., 1970.

Radin, Dean. *The Conscious Universe: The Scientific Truth of Psychic Phenomena.* New York: HarperCollins, 1997.

Sanders, Pete, Jr., *You Are Psychic: The Free Soul Method.* New York: Fawcett Columbine Book, 1989.

Schwartz, Gary. *The Afterlife Experiments: Breakthrough Scientific Evidence of Life after Death.* New York: Pocket Books, 2002.

————. *The Living Energy Universe.* Charlottesville, Virginia: Hampton Roads Publishing Company, 1999.

Sheldrake, Rupert. *Dogs That Know When Their Owners Are Coming Home: And Other Unexplained Powers of Animals.* New York. Crown Publishers, 1999.

Targ, Russell and Keith Harary. *The Mind Race: Understanding and Using Psychic Ability.* New York: Random House, 1984.

Targ, Russell and Jane Katra, Ph.D. *Miracles of the Mind: Exploring Nonlocal Consciousness and Spiritual Healing.* Novato, Calif.: New World Library, 1999.

ANIMAL HEALTH AND TRAINING

Billinghurst, Ian. *Give Your Dog a Bone.* Lithgow, N.S.W., Australia: Self-published, 1993.

Donaldson, Jean. *Dogs Are from Neptune.* Montreal, Quebec: Lasar Multi-Media Productions, 1998.

Frazier, Anita. *New Natural Cat: A Complete Guide for Finicky Owners.* New York: E. P. Dutton, 1990.

Frost, April and Rondi Lightmark. *Beyond Obedience: Training with Awareness for You and Your Dog.* New York: Harmony Books, 1998.

Goldstein, Martin, D.V.M. *The Nature of Animal Healing: The Path to Your Pet's Health, Happiness and Longevity.* New York: Knopf, 1999.

Kaminski, Patricia and Richard Katz. *Flower Essence Repertory: A Comprehensive Guide to North American and English Flower Essences for Emotional and Spiritual Well-Being.* Nevada City, Calif.: The Flower Essence Society, 1996.

Martin, Ann and Michael Fox. *Foods Pets Die For: Shocking Facts about Pet Food.* Troutdale, Oreg.: NewSage Press, 1997.

McConnell, Patricia. *Cautious Canine.* Berkeley, Calif.: James & Kenneth Publishers, Dog's Best Friend, Ltd., 1998.

Pryor, Karen. *Don't Shoot the Dog: The New Art of Teaching and Training.* New York: Bantam Books, 1984.

Schoen, Allen, D.V.M. *Love, Miracles, and Animal Healing: A Heartwarming*

Look at the Spiritual Bond between Animals and Humans. New York: Fireside, 1995.

Schultze, Kymythy. *Natural Nutrition for Dogs and Cats: The Ultimate Pet Diet.* Carlsbad, Calif.: Hay House, 1998.

Schwartz, Cheryl. *Four Paws, Five Directions.* Berkeley, Calif.: Celestial Arts, 1996.

Self, Hilary Page. *A Modern Horse Herbal.* Buckingham, UK: Kenilworth Press, 1996.

Tellington-Jones, Linda. *Getting in Touch with Your Dog: A Gentle Approach to Influencing Behavior, Health and Performance.* North Pomfret, Vt.: Trafalgar Square Publishing, 2001.

———. *Improve Your Horse's Well-Being: A Step-by-Step Guide to TTouch and TTeam Training.* North Pomfret, Vt.: Traflagar Square Publishing, 2001.

The Whole Horse Journal: Though this is no longer published, you can order back issues by calling: 800-424-7887.

NATURE

Buhner, Stephen. *The Lost Language of Plants: The Ecological Importance of Plant Medicines to Life on Earth.* White River Junction, Vt.: Chelsea Green Publishing, 2002.

De Quincey, Christian. *Radical Nature: Rediscovering the Soul of Matter.* Montpelier, Vt.: Invisible Cities Press, 2002.

Hill, Julia Butterfly. *The Legacy of Luna: The Story of a Tree, a Woman, and the Struggle to Save the Redwoods.* San Francisco: HarperSanFrancisco, 2001.

Hogan, Linda and Brenda Peterson. *The Sweet Breathing of Plants: Women Writing on the Green World.* New York: North Point Press, 2001.

Johnson, Buffie. *Lady of the Beasts: The Goddess and Her Sacred Animals.* Rochester, Vt.: Inner Traditions International, 1994.

Macy, Joanna. *World As Lover, World As Self.* Berkeley, Calif.: Parallax Press, 1991.

McLuhan, T. C. *Touch the Earth: A Self-Portrait of Indian Existence.* New York: Simon & Schuster, 1971.

Seed, John and Joanna Macy. *Thinking Like a Mountain: Toward a Council of All Beings.* Gabriola Island, British Columbia: New Society Publishers, 1988.

Skafte, Dianne, Ph.D. *When Oracles Speak: Understanding the Signs and Symbols All around Us.* Wheaton, Ill.: Quest Books, 2000.

Tompkins, Peter and Christopher Bird. *The Secret Life of Plants.* New York: HarperCollins, 1973.

MEDICAL INTUITION AND ENERGY HEALING

Brennan, Barbara. *Hands of Light: A Guide to Healing through the Human Energy Field.* New York: Bantam, 1993.

Doi, Hiroshi. *Modern Reiki Methods for Healing.* Coquitlan, British Columbia: Fraser Journal Publications, 2000.

Dossey, Larry. *Healing Words: The Power of Prayer and the Practice of Medicine.* New York: HarperCollins, 1997.

———. *Prayer Is Good Medicine: How to Reap the Healing Benefits of Prayer.* New York: HarperCollins, 1997.

Ingerman, Sandra. *Medicine for the Earth: How to Transform Personal and Environmental Toxins.* New York: Three Rivers Press, 2000.

———. *Soul Retrieval: Mending the Fragmented Self through Shamanic Practice.* San Francisco: HarperSanFrancisco, 1991.

Motz, Julie. *Hands of Life.* New York: Bantam, 1998.

PallasDowney, Rhonda. *The Complete Book of Flower Essences: 48 Natural and Beautiful Ways to Heal Yourself and Your Life.* Novato, Calif.: New World Library, 2002.

Schultz, Mona Lisa. *Awakening Intuition: Using Your Mind-Body Network for Insight and Healing.* New York: Harmony Books, 1998.

Wilde, Claire. *Hands On Energy Therapy for Horses and Riders.* North Pomfret, Vt.: Trafalgar Square Publishing, 1999.

ETHICS AND THE ROOTS OF THE ECOLOGICAL CRISIS

Eisler, Riane. *The Chalice and the Blade: Our History, Our Future.* San Francisco: HarperSanFrancisco, 1988.

———. *The Power of Partnership: The Seven Relationships That Will Change Your Life.* Novato, Calif.: New World Library, 2002.

Gimbutas, Marija. *The Civilization of the Goddess.* San Francisco: HarperSanFrancisco, 1991.

Jensen, Derrick. *A Language Older Than Words.* New York: Context Books, 2000.

Marler, Joan, ed. *From the Realm of the Ancestors: An Anthology in Honor of Marija Gimbutas.* Manchester, Conn.: Knowledge, Ideas and Trends, 1997.

Regenstein, Lewis. *The Politics of Extinction: The Shocking Story of the World's Endangered Animals.* Houndsmills, Basingstoke Hampshire, UK: Macmillan Publishers Ltd., 1975.

Roszak, Theodore. *The Voice of the Earth: An Exploration of Ecopsychology.* Grand Rapids, Mich.: Phanes Press, Inc., 2001.

Singer, Peter. *Animal Liberation.* New York: Ecco Press, 2001.

Sjoo, Monica. *Return of the Dark/Light Mother or New Age Armageddon?* Austin, Tex.: Plain View Press, 1999.

Stone, Christopher. *Should Trees Have Standing? And Other Essays on Laws, Morals and the Environment.* Dobbs Ferry, N.Y.: Oceana Publications, 1996.

Weisberg, Barry. *Beyond Repair: The Ecology of Capitalism.* Boston: Beacon Press, 1971.

Resources

Useful
Web Sites

ALTERNATIVE/HOLISTIC VETERINARIANS

Here are two Web sites that will help you find a holistic veterinarian in your state:

American Academy of Veterinary Acupuncturists:

www.aava.org

American Holistic Veterinary Medical Association:

www.ahvma.org

CAT FENCING

There are many types of fence that you can install to keep your cat in your backyard, patio, or deck and keep other animals out. Look at the Web site listed below to see an example of one kind of fencing. Then do a search on the Internet to find the right kind of fencing for you and your cat. They can be reached at:

www.catfencein.com

CLICKER TRAINING

Clicker training is a nonviolent form of training. Check out the Web sites below to find a clicker trainer in your area.
Karen Pryor's site on clicker training for dogs:

www.clickertraining.com

Alexandra Kurland's site on clicker training for horses:

www.theclickercenter.com

DOG BOOKS

These are two good Web sites for books about dogs:

www.flyingdogpress.com

www.dogwise.com

FLOWER ESSENCES

There are many kinds of flower essences to choose from. For more information, please visit the following Web sites:
Flower Essence Society:

www.fesflowers.com

Desert Flower Essences:

www.desert-alchemy.com

Alaskan Flower Essence Project:

www.alaskanessences.com

Living Flower Essences:

www.livingfloweressences.com

LOST ANIMALS

For information on how to search for a lost animal go to:

www.petrescue.com

For help with the search, contact:

Sherlock Bones, a pet detective who will send out flyers or post-cards in your area:

www.sherlockbones.com (800-942-6637)

Pet Finders, a service that will telephone people within your area:

www.petfindersalert.com (800-274-2556)

International K9 Search and Rescue, a group that will search for your lost animal using a trained search-and-rescue dog:

www.k9sardog.com

NUTRITIONAL SUPPLEMENT SUPPLIERS

Dogs and Cats

www.all-the-best.com

www.drgoodpet.com

Horses

www.dropinthebucket.com

http://figuerola-laboratories.com

www.hiltonherbs.com

www.thehorsehoof.com

http://vitaroyal.com

TTEAM AND TTOUCH

These are the unique, nonviolent animal training and bodywork methods developed by Linda Tellington-Jones:

www.tteam-ttouch.com

Index

S

About the Author

Marta Williams got her undergraduate degree in natural resource conservation at the University of California in Berkeley and her master's degree in biology at San Francisco State University. Before becoming an animal communicator, she worked for many years as a wildlife biologist and environmental scientist. Marta works with clients all over the world, providing intuitive consultations for all types of animals. She lives in Northern California and travels internationally to lecture, teach classes, and hold clinics on intuitive communication with animals and nature. To schedule a consultation or to find out about attending or hosting a class or clinic, please visit her website at www.martawilliams.com.